HOW TO DESIGN 3D GAMES WITH WEB TECHNOLOGY - BOOK 01

Three.js – HTML5 and WebGL

Jordi Josa

THE FIVE PLANETS

Index of contents

INTRODUCTION **9**

Who this book is for 9

Purpose of this collection 9

Let's create our role-playing game 9

  Why a role-playing game? 9

  What will the game we create be like? 10

Technologies used 13

  Three.js 13

  Collision detection and laws of physics 13

    Ammo.js 13

    Cannon.js 14

    Physijs 14

    Oimo.js 14

  JQuery 14

  Blender 14

  Adobe Photoshop 14

C1 - THREE.JS: FIRST STEPS **17**

"Hello, World!" program..17

Scene 19

Mesh 19

  Geometry..20

  Materials..22

Camera...22

  Perspective Camera (THREE.PrespectiveCamera)....................23

Render 25

  WebGL (THREE.WebGLRenderer) 26

  Canvas (THREE.CanvasRenderer) 26

  CSS3D (THREE.CSS3DRenderer)...................................26

Axes, Position, Scale and Rotation...27

Axes 27

Position and Scale 27

    Relative Position 28

Rotation 29

    Rotation on its axis 29

    Rotation in respect to a reference point 30

    Converting degrees to radians and vice versa 31

Animation of the Scene 31

Clock 32

C2 - TREEJS: PREPARING THE DEVELOPMENT ENVIRONMENT .. 35

Solving the "cross-origin-domain" error 35

    Chrome 36

    Firefox 36

Installing a local web server 37

    Portable servers 38

        PWS (Apache + MySQL + PHP) 38

        UwAmp (Apache + MySQL + PHP) 38

        Mongose 38

    Non-portable servers 38

        XAMPP 38

        MAMP 39

        Web server for Node.js 39

Statistics (stats.js) 40

UI Control 41

    Field types to use in the interface 43

    Folders 45

    Events 45

Detecting WebGL support 46

C3 - THREEJS: GEOMETRIES, MATERIALS, LIGHTS AND SHADOWS 47

geometries 47

    Predefined 3D geometries 47

Cube (THREE.BoxGeometry) 47

Sphere (THREE.Sphere) 47

Polyhedron (THREE. IcosahedronGeometry, THREE.DodecahedronGeometry, THREE.OctahedronGeometry, THREE.TetrahedronGeometry) 48

Cylinder (THREE.CylinderGeometry) 49

Cone (THREE.ConeGeometry) 49

Torus (THREE.TorusGeometry) 49

TorusKnot (THREE.TorusKnotGeometry) 50

Predefined 2D geometries 50

Plane (THREE.Plane) 50

Circle and polygon (THREE.Circle) 50

Ring (THREE.Ring) 51

Customised geometries 51

Free 2D figure (THREE.Shape and THREE.ShapeGeometry) 51

Giving volume to a flat figure (THREE.ExtrudeGeometry) 53

3D text (THREE.TextGeometry) 54

Materials 56

THREE.MeshBasicMaterial 56

THREE.MeshNomalMaterial 57

THREE.MeshDepthMaterial 58

THREE.MeshLambertMaterial 59

THREE.MeshPhongMaterial 60

THREE.MultiMaterial 61

Textures 63

Multiple textures - UV Mapping 64

Repeating texture 70

Transparencies 73

Lights 76

Ambient (THREE.AmbientLight) and directional (THREE.DirectionalLight) lighting 76

Hemispheric light (THREE.HemisphereLight) 79

Point Light (THREE.PointLight) and Spot Light (THREE.SpotLight) 81

Shadows 84

C4 - THREEJS: CREATING OUR WORLD **89**

Load external models (loaders) 89

Format .OBJ (THREE.OBJLoader and THREE.MTLLoader) 90

Enabling shadows and changing object properties 92

Solving problems 94

Scale 94

Troubleshoot problems with the web server 94

The object is not displaying the texture. 94

Slow loading time or a reduction of frames during running. 95

Textures, range, colours 96

Collada fromat .DAE (THREE.ColladaLoader) and object animations 96

Activation of object animation 99

Enabling shadows and changing object properties 99

Solving problems 100

Scale 100

Troubleshoot problems with the web server 101

The object is not displaying the texture. 101

Slow loading time or a reduction of frames during running. 101

Native format of three.js 102

Fog 104

Linear fog - THREE.Fog (colour, start, end) 105

Exponential fog - THREE.FoxExp2 (colour, density) 105

Creating the base for the game 106

Improving the animation loop (world_v01.js) 109

Methods of $WORLD 110

Properties of $WORLD 110

Creating the base ground (ground_v01.js) 112

Moving an object along a set path (controls_path_v01.js) 114

Creating a sky 117

Creating the sky with a cube (Skybox) 117

Creating a sky with a sphere (Skydome) 122

Creating a sky with a sphere and a gradient of colours............................124

Creating vegetation and natural elements 126

Using THREE.Sprite to create grass and trees................................127

Creating grass using planes 130

Creating the game map... 132

Loading multiple non-animated models simultaneously 136

Cloning objects..137

Creating a progress bar and a loading screen (SplashScreen)....................142

Adding villagers and creating their daily routines 147

Cloning animated objects 149

Creating basic Artificial Intelligence through pre-established routes........151

Adding monsters and moving them 153

Creating basic Artificial Intelligence through unpredictable movement ... 154

C5 - THREEJS: EXPLORING AND INTERACTING................157

First-person basic controller – Movement with keyboard and mouse 157

Three.js controllers... 161

FirstPersonControls.js 161

FlyControls.js 162

OrbitControls.js 162

TrackballControls.js 163

Controlling movement via webcam (WebRTC) 163

Access to the webcam (HTML5 getUserMedia API) 164

Creating the interface 165

Capturing the two images..166

Comparing the last two frames of the camera............................167

Determining the buttons or screen areas that show movement....................169

Applying movement control to the game................................170

Controling webpages with games console control pads................................. 171

API Detection 172

Gamepad Events..172

Get the list of objects of gamepad type 173

Complete example: viewing gamepad status 175

Putting it all together 178

Selecting and clicking on objects - raycaster..............................179

How does it work?... 179

Preparing the scene 180

Projecting the line 182

Calculating intersections and selecting the object 183

Clicking on the object 184

Drag and drop - raycaster 184

Preparing the scene 185

Controlling mouse events 188

interacting with THE game elements 190

Full screen (HTML5 Fullscreen API).....................................195

Methods, properties and Fullscreen API events 195

Availability detection of the full screen API 196

Changing to full screen mode 197

Cancelling full screen mode 197

Verifying if full screen mode is active 198

Capturing full screen events 198

CSS pseudo-class :fullscreen 199

C6 THREEJS: UPCOMING BOOKS IN THE COLLECTION................ 201

Management of collision detection... 201

Motor of physical laws 201

Creating a rich interface for the game 202

Management of sound effects and background music........................ 202

How to store and retrieve data items 203

How to package and distribute our application 203

Improving the Artificial Intelligence of monsters and villagers................ 203

Sharders, advanced textures and particle system.......................... 204

3D animated models 204

INTRODUCTION

WHO THIS BOOK IS FOR

This book is aimed at people who know the basics of JavaScript and HTML, want to learn how to create *3D* animations and scenes using the library *Three.js*, and want to enter the world of web game design. Furthermore, this book is part of a collection, which introduces all the concepts, tools and technologies needed to create complex games and become a true game design master.

Throughout this collection of books, we'll design and install a role-playing game called "***THE FIVE PLANETS***". Therefore, this book is also intended for those who already know how to use *Three.js*. but want to continue the process of creating this game, and want to learn about more complex elements of game design that occur in later stages.

PURPOSE OF THIS COLLECTION

The aim of this book collection is to teach you everything you need to know about creating 3D games with web technology and finally to propose ways to monetise the games you create. To do this we'll create a role-playing game from scratch, which is like games like "*The Elder Scrolls V: Skyrim*" or "*Fallout 4*". Therefore, the game we create will also include the main features these games have, which include creating 3D maps, artificial enemy intelligence, inventory management (weapons, armour and potions), a mission system and of course statistics and system levels.

It's likely that we won't include all the aspects I mentioned above in the RPG we're going to create. This is because we don't have the budget nor the equipment that so many complex games require. However, the game we create will be a mixture of old games, like "*Ishar III*" or the legendary saga "*Migth and Magic*", and newer games.

LET'S CREATE OUR ROLE-PLAYING GAME

Why a role-playing game?

Creating a 3D role-playing game presents a series of challenges that don't crop up in platform games, arcade games or board games. Everything is much simpler in these types of games, because they only cover a small range of features.

On the other hand, RPGs, or at least the ones we have in mind, incorporate the following elements:

• Large maps, which include cities, forests, plains and of course dungeons that players can interact with. This broadly covers designing 3D maps and scenes as well as examining basic techniques in order to create the sky and the ground.

• A real time "*shooter*", with the ability to cast devastating spells such as fireballs. In these types of games, we face a horde of enemies who can respond with equally formidable attacks. This will allow us to work with artificial intelligence and advanced animations.

• These games are usually long and last for several days, and have many missions and changing worlds. All this means that saving a game, uploading the data and then returning to the same point at which we left the game involves handling a lot of data. This gives us the opportunity to use different web data storage techniques.

• These games usually have an elaborate plot during the game, including cinematic scenes and performances to reinforce the story. Some even incorporate risqué scenes: who doesn't remember the legendary "*Dragon Age*", which allowed characters to enter into romantic relationships? This will allow us to intensively use cameras in our game scenes.

• Another feature is that they have an *Interface* and a developed menu system: the mission diary, the records of the characters, inventory management screens, maps, among others. This will allow us to show different techniques of how to integrate the UI (user interface) and make it interact with the 3D world.

• The characters have multiple attributes and skills to manage when they level up. As they progress they gain strength, magical ability and skills that require more complex enemies and challenges. This point will allow us to explain how to level the playing field in order to maintain interest in the game.

• And if that is not enough, there are usually a host of elements that players can interact with such as secret passages, levers, boxes, plants, books, etc.

Therefore, we believe that this type of game is a very wise choice as a means of acquiring knowledge in web game design.

What will the game we create be like?

The game is quite advanced early on in the book as we've already assembled the majority of the *interface,* the collision detection system and a first map of the city, where our heroes begin their adventure.

Completing a project of this size clearly goes beyond the capacity of one person, so I don't intend to finish it on my own. Instead, I would be happy to create the first level of the game, then let my readers finish creating the game. Below I've attached some screenshots of the components created in the game to give you a taste of what's to come, and arouse your interest in the following collection of books.

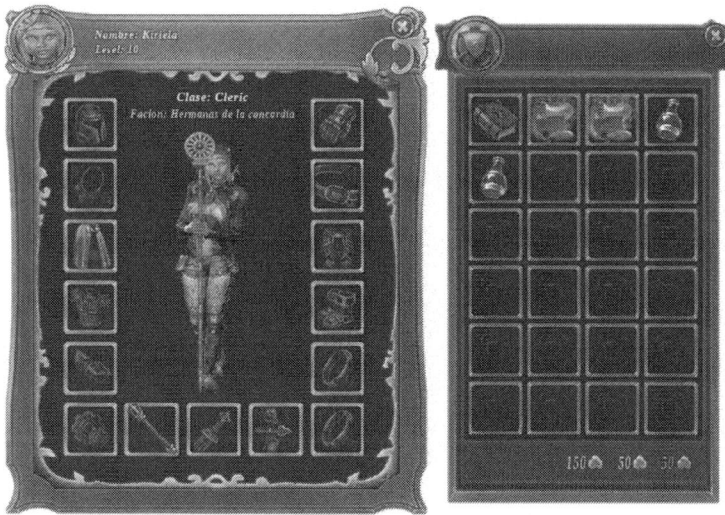

Fig. I-01 Example of the character Kiriela and the inventory.

Fig. I-03 Image of the initial city.

Fig. I-4 Example of one of the monsters of the game edited with the application Blender.

Fig. I-5 Example of the collision detection system.

Fig. I-5 Example of the input interface.

TECHNOLOGIES USED

Three.js

Three.js is a library written in JavaScript to create and display *3D* animated graphics in a web browser. You can see examples of it and download it here: http://threejs.org.

This library was created and released on *GitHub* by Ricardo Cabello in April 2010, known by his pseudonym Mr. Doob. Over time it has become one of the most important and popular libraries to use for creating animations on *WebGL*. Today there are more than 390 collaborators who are responsible for improving it.

Collision detection and laws of physics

When developing games, or certain scenes, it's necessary to simulate how the laws of physics affect the objects in question. To do this, we must consider parameters such as gravity, acceleration, volume, speed, weight or whether the surfaces are slippery or rough. We also should determine what happens when two objects collide. For instance, we would have to consider what would happen when fireballs thrown by wizards hits enemies. Luckily, we have several JavaScript libraries that carry out many of these calculations for us.

Ammo.js

Ammo.js is based on the *BulletPhysics library* (http://bulletphysics.org/) written in *C++*. The source code has been directly translated to JavaScript without human intervention, so that the functionality is identical to the original. However, its performance is affected by the differences between programming languages.

Cannon.js

Cannon.js is a library created directly in JavaScript and is inspired by *ammo.js*. It performs lightly better because it is written directly with JavaScript. You can see examples of it and download it at http://cannonjs.org.

Physijs

Physijs is built on top of the *ammo.js* library. However, there is also a *cannon.js* branch of *Physijs*. It allows physical simulation in a separate thread (via *"Webworker"*) to avoid an impact on the performance of calculations in the application and to speed up 3D rendering. You can see examples of it and download it at http://chandlerprall.github.io/Physijs/

Oimo.js

Oimo.js, like the previous two libraries, is a physics simulation engine for rigid objects. This is a complete conversion of JavaScript *OimoPhysics* originally created for *ActionScript* 3.0. You can see examples of it and download it at https://github.com/lo-th/Oimo.js/

JQuery

JQuery is a JavaScript library that makes it easier to interact with HTML documents. It has methods to manipulate the *DOM* tree, handle events, develop and implement animations, and use *AJAX functions* on web pages.

In some of our examples we'll use *JQuery* to implement the game's menus and sub-screens, such as the inventory, the quest log window, or popup message boxes. You can see examples of *JQuery* and download it at https://jquery.com/

Blender

Blender is a software platform, dedicated especially to modelling, lighting, rendering, animating and creating three-dimensional graphics. In this collection of books, we'll use it to modify and create objects in *3D* and to animate the monsters and characters in the game.

The application is free and currently supports *Windows, Mac, Linux* (including *Android) Solaris, FreeBSD and IRIX.* You can see examples of it and download it at https://www.blender.org/

Adobe Photoshop

You will need a good graphics editor during the game making process. This will help us create and edit the textures of objects and characters and to create the graphical interface of the game.

Correcting palettes, replacing one colour with another or adjusting image sizes to be small enough for the website will be basic tasks when preparing objects for the game. Therefore, it's essential to have a good editor that allows you to do all this comfortably. I've personally used *Photoshop* for this book, because it's one of the most complete and functional graphics editors on the market. Unfortunately, it's the only tool we'll use that isn't free.

C1 - THREE.JS: FIRST STEPS

In this chapter, we'll address the most basic elements of *Three.js* and create our first scene.

"HELLO, WORLD!" PROGRAM

Modern browsers incorporate features for composing *2D* and *3D* images.

Three.js is a JavaScript library that makes it easier to develop *3D* scenes, by using a layer to overcome the problem of small implementation differences that exist between different browsers. For this book, we used version 80, which you can download on this page: http://threejs.org.

We'll start off by creating a scene that shows a cube rotating and moving horizontally. This example will introduce you to the most basic elements of the library. Remember you can download the sample code in this book: https://www.thefiveplanets.org/blog/book01.

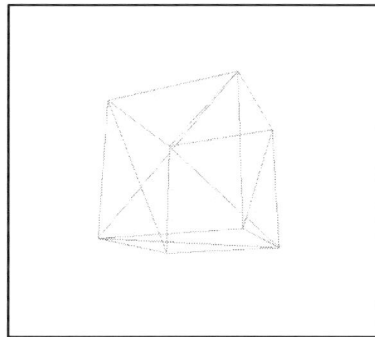

Fig. 1.1 Rotating Cube.

The complete code to create our scene is as follows.

```
<!DOCTYPE html>
<html>
<head>
<meta charset="utf-8">
  <style>
    body {
      background-color: #ffffff;
      margin: 0;
      overflow: hidden;
    }
  </style>
</head>
<body>
```

```
<script src="https://ajax.googleapis.com/ajax/libs/threejs/r76/three.min.js "></script>
<script>
   var camera, scene, renderer;
   var geometry, material, mesh;
   var clock;

     function init() {
        renderer = new THREE.WebGLRenderer();
        renderer.setSize( window.innerWidth, window.innerHeight );
        document.body.appendChild( renderer.domElement );

        scene = new THREE.Scene();

        geometry = new THREE.CubeGeometry( 1, 1, 1 );
        material = new THREE.MeshBasicMaterial(
            {color: 0xff0000, wireframe: true});

        mesh = new THREE.Mesh( geometry, material );
        scene.add( mesh );

        camera = new THREE.PerspectiveCamera(
            75,window.innerWidth/window.innerHeight,0.1,100 );
        camera.position.set(0,0,-3);
        camera.lookAt(mesh.position);

        clock = new THREE.Clock();
        window.addEventListener( 'resize', onWindowResize, false );
     }
     var dir=1;
     function animate() {
        requestAnimationFrame( animate );

        var delta =  clock.getDelta();

        mesh.rotation.x += delta * 0.5;
        mesh.rotation.y += delta * 2;
        mesh.position.x += dir*delta;
        if (mesh.position.x > 2) {
           dir=-1;
        } else if (mesh.position.x < - 2)  {
           dir=1;
        }
        renderer.render( scene, camera );
     }

     function onWindowResize() {
```

```
        windowHalfX = window.innerWidth / 2;
        windowHalfY = window.innerHeight / 2;
        camera.aspect = window.innerWidth /window.innerHeight;
        camera.updateProjectionMatrix();
        renderer.setSize( window.innerWidth, window.innerHeight );
    }

    init();
    animate();

</script>
</body>
</html>
```

You can use the following link to download the sample code and see how it works:

http://www.thefiveplanets.org/b01/c01/01-hello-threejs.html

When you run the sample, you'll see a square with red edges rotating on itself and moving from right to left and vice versa. So, let us look at the various elements of the example.

SCENE

The scene is the composition of the world we want to show. We'll add all the elements that comprise it which are:

- 3D objects;
- the camera or camera through which to see the world;
- the light spots or lights that illuminate the scene;
- sounds and atmospheric music;
- and configuring special effects such as fog.

The instruction to create it is:

`scene = new THREE.Scene();`

MESH

3D objects to add to the scene are called *Mesh*. In this case, the object is a cube.

Every object is composed of at least its geometry (shape) and its material, which specifies its colour, its textures, or even how the lighting affects it.

`geometry = new THREE.CubeGeometry( 1, 1, 1 );`

```
material = new THREE.MeshBasicMaterial({
    color: 0xff0000,
    wireframe: true});
mesh = new THREE.Mesh( geometry, material );
scene.add( mesh );
```

Mesh can also consist of information about how the object should be animated. For example, a character such as a farmer could contain the sequence of animations for walking, running, working, fighting, etc., which specify what shape he should take to create the sensation of movement.

Geometry

Geometries are instances of **THREE.Geometry** and are made up of vertices and faces. Vertices are instances of **THREE.Vector3** and represent points in three-dimensional space, while faces are triangles that link three points and are instances of **THREE.Face3**. For example, a sphere is a collection of triangles linked together. For instance, a cube has 8 vertices and 12 triangles (*faces*) and each side of the cube is made up of two triangles.

In the following links, we see the cube with its faces and vertices highlighted. In the first link the vertices are highlighted with red dots. In the second, the faces are painted in different colours.

Vertices: https://www.thefiveplanets.org/b01/c01/02-vertices.html

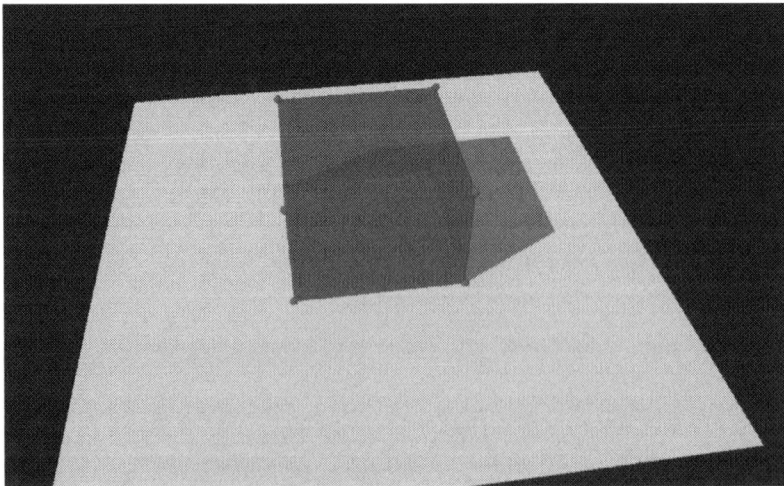

Fig. 1.2 Showing the vertices of a cube.

Faces: https://www.thefiveplanets.org/b01/c01/03-faces.html

Fig. 1.3 Showing the faces of a cube.

In the following example, we see the representation of a flat triangle.

```
var geometry = new THREE.Geometry();
geometry.vertices.push(
    new THREE.Vector3( -1, 1, 0 ),
    new THREE.Vector3( -1, -1, 0 ),
    new THREE.Vector3( 1, -1, 0 )
);
geometry.faces.push(
    new THREE.Face3( 0, 1, 2 )
);
var material = new THREE.MeshNormalMaterial();
var mesh = new THREE.Mesh( geometry, material );
scene.add( mesh );
```

Use the following link to view the code running:
https://www.thefiveplanets.org/b01/c01/04-geometry.html.

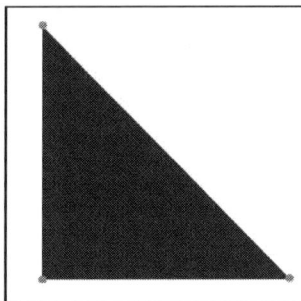
Fig. 1.4 Triangle with vertices represented by a red circle.

Normally, we rarely define the geometries manually. Fortunately, *Three.js* includes many shapes such as cubes, spheres, cylinders, and planes by default. In chapter two you can see a full list of these shapes.

Blender is a free editor that lets you create shapes at an advanced level and export them in formats that can be used directly in *Three.js*.

Materials

Materials are "*the skin*" of the shapes. Furthermore, they define the colour of each face of a shape, how light acts on each face, or if both sides or only one is visible. As with shapes, *Three.js* provides a rich collection of classes to create different types of materials according to the effect we want to generate, such as creating materials that ignore the light.

In the first example, we've used the most basic material **THREE.MeshBasicMaterial**, and have set the colour red and the property *wireframe* to *true* so that, instead of painting the faces with a solid colour, we create lines between the vertices.

```
material = new THREE.MeshBasicMaterial({
    color: 0xff0000, wireframe: true}
);
```

Some properties that you can experiment with are *transparent* with value *true* and *opacity* to specify the degree of transparency of the layers.

An important property that you should know about is *side,* which enables you to specify which face is shown. Typically, for performance reasons, only the faces of the object that we know will be displayed are painted. For example, if we're not going to focus on the interior of a closed cube then we'll only show the outer faces.

The three possible values for this property are: **THREE.FrontSide**, in front; **THREE.BackSide**, behind; and **THREE.DoubleSide** on both sides. Showing the front or back face does not depend on the position of the camera but depends on the order of its vertices. The front face corresponds to the direction anti-clockwise. If we use *THREE.DoubleSide* it will always be visible, regardless of where we place the camera.

CAMERA

The cameras, the eyes with which we see the world, are not represented graphically. A scene can contain as many cameras as you want, but there can only be one of them active to visualize the world. However, you can switch from one camera to another without any limitations.

You can rotate and position the cameras, but the result of such changes will only be seen by calling the method *render*, as we've seen in the previous examples.

There are two types of projections that we can use when creating the camera:

The perspective projection (***THREE.PrespectiveCamera***) deforms the objects according to their distance and position relative to the camera, as events occur in real time. It's typically used in first-person games.

Isometric projection (***THREE.OrthographicCamera***) is a perspective that respects the size of objects, regardless of how far they are from the camera (2.5D). It's often used in games like "*Diablo*" and many role-play games designed in HTML.

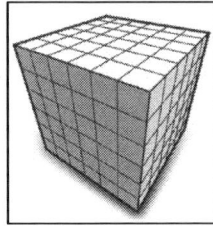

Fig. 1.5 Perspective projection.

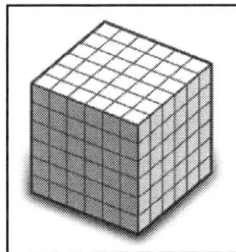

Fig. 1.6 Isometric projection.

Perspective Camera (THREE.PrespectiveCamera)

The four parameters of the perspective camera used in the initial example are:

```
camera = new THREE.PerspectiveCamera(
    75, window.innerWidth/window.innerHeight, 0.1, 100);
```

Bearing in mind these four parameters we observe this figure.

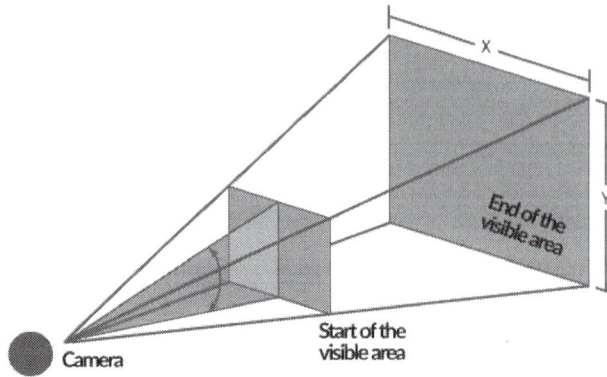

Fig. 1.7 Camera parameters.

- The first parameter (**75**) defines the vertical visual field of the camera in degrees (from bottom up). This is the extent of the observable world that is seen on the screen at any given time. The horizontal visual field is calculated with the vertical.
- The second parameter (***window.innerWidth/window.innerHeight***) defines the aspect ratio of the camera. Usually the width of the window divided by its height is used, otherwise the picture is distorted.
- The third parameter (***0.1***) defines the start of the visible area. In other words, objects between the camera and the specified distance are not visible. In the example the distance is virtually zero.
- The last parameter (***100***) defines the end of the visible area. In the example, when an object exceeds 100 units it will be outside the visible area of the camera and the only part that's within the area will be displayed.

Other important properties of the camera are its position and the point of the scene to be focused on. All objects (cameras, shapes and lights) and scenes that we create have a property called ***position***, which contains an instance of a vector (***THREE.Vector3***). To specify the position of the camera, simply run the method ***set*** from ***THREE.Vector3***, using the coordinates (*X, Y and Z*) as parameters.

camera.position.set (0,0,-3);

To rotate the camera, we can use the method ***lookAt*** to focus on a particular point. This method will only work if the camera has been added directly to the scene and not an object.

camera.lookAt(mesh.position);

To see the two camera types working, you can use the link below. In the example, we can switch from one perspective to another.

https://www.thefiveplanets.org/b01/c01/05-camera.html

RENDER

At this point we have everything ready to display an attractive 3D scene. Now we only need to specify the part of the website where we'll draw our composition. For this we'll use "*renders*", which are responsible for creating the DOM element (*WebGL, Canvas or CSS3*), and then we'll add it on the page.

```
renderer = new THREE.WebGLRenderer();
renderer.setSize( window.innerWidth, window.innerHeight );
renderer.setClearColor(new THREE.Color(0xEEEEEE, 1.0));
document.body.appendChild( renderer.domElement );
```

To create a *render,* we need to specify at least the following properties:

1. The size it will be measured in pixels. In the example, we used the width and height of the window (*window.innerWidth, window.innerHeight*).
2. The background colour used by *Three.js*. To specify the colour, we can also specify opacity. In our case, we've specified a solid colour (1.0).

The *render* creates an element of *HTML5* of a *CANVAS* type that we must add to our website. We can add it directly to the body of the document (***document.body.appendChild***) or create a layer (***div***) with a "*id*" so that it can be referenced.

```
document.getElementById("id").appendChild(render.domElement);
```

Every time we want the changes made in the scene to be reflected on the screen we must use the *render* method:

```
render.render(escena, camara);
```

As parameters, we specify: the scene we want to render and the camera. Obviously, the same scene will look different depending on the position occupied by the camera and the direction in which it's focused.

Tip

Using several *renders*, one on top of the other, marking the background colour as transparent, can improve performance. For example, the character animations could be included in the *render* above, while the *render* below would represent the background.

WebGL *(THREE.WebGLRenderer)*

This is the kind of *render* we used in the first example, and which we'll use regularly. To represent the scenes, it uses *APIs* from *WebGL* present in modern browsers. Of all the *renders* available, *THREE.WebGLRenderer* is the only one that allows us to create advanced effects for shadows and highlights.

Canvas *(THREE.CanvasRenderer)*

CanvasRenderer uses *APIs* from Canvas 2D without using *WebGL*. This implies that a wider range of devices and browsers can be reached for simple scenes. However, it's much slower because it doesn't benefit from hardware acceleration offered by *WebGL APIs*.

We won't use CanvasRender for the game we're creating, since we need to access all optimization techniques for this kind of game.

You can see an example CanvasRender on the following link:

https://www.thefiveplanets.org/b01/c01/06-canvasrenderer.html

CSS3D *(THREE.CSS3DRenderer)*

Combining HTML and CSS offers more and more possibilities. The latest versions of CSS support 3D transformations, which means that we can use CSS styles to transform our WEB pages into 3D objects.

Fig. 1.8 Example of CSS3DRenderer.

Unlike the other two *renders, CCS3D* doesn't use the HTML CANVAS element. Instead, styles and CSS transformations are directly applied to html elements. Obviously, this render offers different possibilities from those that the other two offer.

You can see the result of applying this technology to a simple web page with a form in the following link: http://www.thefiveplanets.org/b01/c01/07-css3drenderer.html

The *render* isn't included in the library folder but is directly attached as an example, so you can download it on the following website:

https://raw.githubusercontent.com/mrdoob/three.js/master/examples/js/renderers/CSS3DRenderer.js

AXES, POSITION, SCALE AND ROTATION

Axes

Three.js uses a right-hand coordinate system. The device screen coincides with the *xy* plane and the positive z-axis points off screen, towards the observer's eyes.

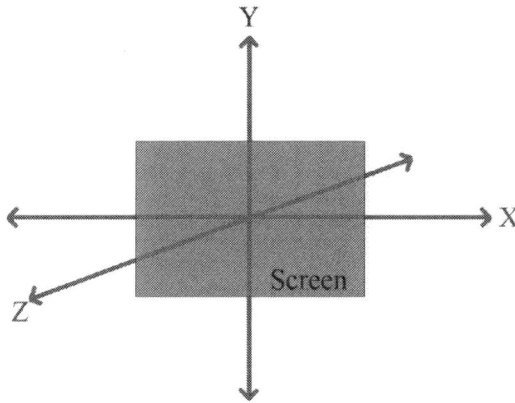

Fig. 1.9 Coordenadas

When an *Three.js* object is added within a scene, it's positioned (by default) at the origin of the *xyz* coordinate system *(0,0,0)*. Therefore, if you add a camera and a cube to a scene, both will have the position *(0, 0, 0)*. We'll also see the cube from within. In this case, we'll move the camera or the cube, for example:

`camera.position.z = 50`

Position and Scale

One of the many options for changing the position and size of the object are the properties **position** and **scale**. Both are instances of *THREE.Vector3* that are created by indicating a point *(x, y, z)*. For the *position*, the default value is *(0,0,0)*, at the origin of the coordinate system, while for the scale it's *(1,1,1)*, indicating that the object must keep its original size on the three axes. For example, with the coordinate *(1,2,1)* we specify that the object must be twice as high as it originally was, but must be same width and depth. If instead we specify the value *(2,2,2)* we are indicating that the object will be double the size while keeping the same proportions.

```
var vec=new THREE.Vector3(x,y,z)
```

The class *THREE.Vector3* has the following properties that are referenced below. For a complete list please consult the documentation of *Three.js*.

Properties
X: The X value of the vector. Default is 0.
Y: The Y value of the vector. Default is 0.
Z: The Z value of the vector. Default is 0.
Methods
.set (x, y, z): Sets the values for the three axes.
.setX (x): Sets the value for the x-axis.
.setY (y): Sets the value for the y-axis.
.setZ (z): Sets the value for the z-axis.
.copy (v): Copies the values of the passed vector3's x, y and z properties to this vector3.

In the initial example, we directly access the properties to set the values, as this is the easiest way.

```
mesh.position.x += dir*delta;
```

Relative Position

All the objects available to add to the scene (camera, figures, lights and even audio) are instances of **THREE.Object3D**, and have the method **Add** which allows us to add other objects within the parent object. In this case, the position of the child object is relative, not in relation to the global coordinates axis, but to the position of the parent object. The same applies to the scale and rotation.

https://www.thefiveplanets.org/b01/c01/08-hello-threejs-scale.html

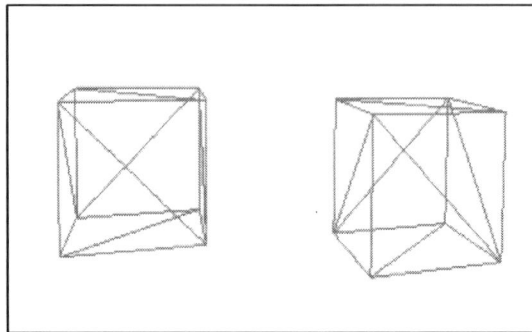

Fig. 1.10 Cube added within another cube.

Rotation

The property "*rotation*" allows us to modify the rotation of an object. Its value is an instance of the class ***THREE.Euler***, defined by indicating the following parameters (*x, y, z, order*). Where "*x*" specifies the radians to be rotated relative to its axis *x*; "*y*" and "*z*" are equal but in respect to their respective axes; and where the *order* deals with the order of rotation. For instance, '*XYZ*' specifies that the object will first be rotated in respect to the *x-axis*, then the *y-axis* and finally the *z-axis*.

```
var eu=new THREE.Euler( 0, 1, 1.57, 'XYZ' );
```

The class *THREE.Vector3* has the following properties. For a complete list, you can consult the documentation of *Three.js*:

Properties
x: X coordinate value.
y: Y coordinate value.
z: Z coordinate value.
order: Order of axes, by default "*XYZ*".

Methods
.set (x, y, z, order): Sets the values for the three axes.
.copy (euler): Copies value of *euler* to this *euler*.

Rotation on its axis

The easiest way to rotate on an axis is copy what we did in the initial example, which is by accessing the properties *x, y, z* of the *rotation* property.

```
mesh.rotation.x += delta * 0.5;
mesh.rotation.y += delta * 2;
```

If we rotate the object on several axes, then we must pay special attention to the order. Turning the object 90° on the *x-axis* and then 90° on *y-axis*, is not the same as doing this the other way around. Note that the order of the instructions will not change the result, because it's the method *render* that will apply the rotation based on the property *order*.

Rotation in respect to a reference point

As we've seen, objects can be added within others, which creates a hierarchy of parents and children objects. Thus, the position of the child object is relative to the centre point of the parent object. If we turn the parent, the child will turn, not on its axis but on the parent's axis. So, to rotate an object on a point, we can simply create an instance of *THREE.Object3D* (without geometry or materials), add the child object to a different position *(0,0,0)*, and turn the parent object.

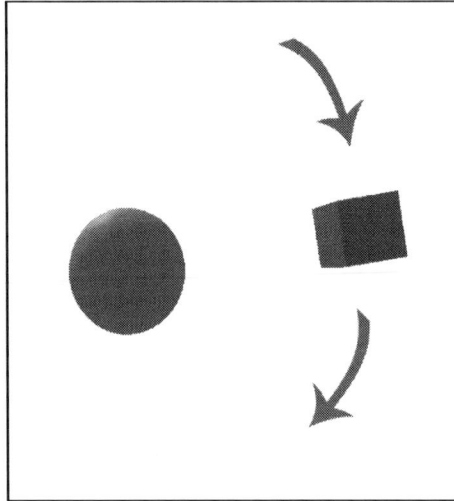

Fig. 1.10 Example of rotation with respect to a reference point.

You can see the example of this in the following:

https://www.thefiveplanets.org/b01/c01/09-rotate-object-around-point.html

The steps we've taken are the following:

1. We create the point on which the object rotates and place it in the designated space.

    ```
    pivotPoint = new THREE.Object3D();
    pivotPoint.position.set(0,0,0);
    scene.add( pivotPoint );
    ```

2. We create the object to rotate.

    ```
    geometry = new THREE.CubeGeometry( 0.5, 0.5, 0.5 );
    material = new THREE.MeshPhongMaterial(
        { color: 0x0000ff}
    ```

```
);
mesh = new THREE.Mesh( geometry, material );
```

3. We add the object to the "*pivotPoint*".

```
pivotPoint.add(mesh);
mesh.position.set(0,2,0);
```

4. We rotate the parent object.

```
pivotPoint.rotation.z += delta * 2;
```

Converting degrees to radians and vice versa

The functions for rotation in *Three.js* use radians, but it's more common to think in *degrees*. To convert degrees to radians we simply need to apply the following formula:

```
radianes = grados*Math.PI/180;
```

Fortunately, *Three.js* incorporates the following default functions that perform the calculation for us:

THREE.degToRad (grados): Converts degrees to radians.
THREE.radToDeg (radianes): Converts radians to degrees.

ANIMATION OF THE SCENE

To move the shapes during execution, we merely need to modify its attribute *position* or *rotation,* and then use the method *render* periodically. Animation (such as movies and games) is nothing more than sequences of images that gives a sense of movement when played in sequence quickly. The smoother the change in position and rotation of the figure in each image the more real the animation will be, so a critical factor is the number of frames displayed every second (*FPS*). Films, for example, run at 24 frames. However, Peter Jackson uses 48 frames in *The Hobbit*, and perhaps others copy him. Games, however, must at least use 30 FPS, but it's common that they remain between 50 and 60 FPS.

JavaScript contains the function ***setTimeOut,*** which lets you run a function after a fixed number of milliseconds. Hence, we can create a code to update the scene and run the method *render* and then recursively call *setTimeOut* again so that we create an infinite loop of calls. This same effect can be achieved with the function ***setInverval,*** which allows you to specify a function and a time in milliseconds with how many times it should be repeated.

Both functions have problems for animation, especially ***setInterval***. This is because when this function is run constantly, and if the rendering takes a long time, calls can be produced one after the other without giving time to perform other tasks, causing the system to collapse. Another problem that affects both functions is that they will always be executed regardless of whether the user is viewing another website, or whether the scene is not visible on the screen at that time, which needlessly consumes *CPU* and *GPU* time. This causes greater battery usage, and hence overheating, in phones and laptops, and greater use of computer fans in desktops. Finally, there is the power of the device, which, according to the graphics card and the device type, support a greater, or lesser degree of updates per second. So, this may result in forcing too many attempts at rendering or staying below optimum performance.

Luckily a new *JavaScript* function has been introduced called "***requestAnimationFrame***". This function is like *setTimeout,* but is improved. The function will only run when our *CANVAS* is wholly or partially visible and will finally manage how often the rendering function is ran for us.

```
function animate() {
    requestAnimationFrame( animate );
    ...
    renderer.render( scene, camera );
}
```

In the example, the function that we will run *requestAnimationFrame* is **animate,** which it's invoked by first loading the page with the *onload* event. The function will be run repeatedly from here on out. Note that we increase or decrease the position and angle of rotation in the code, which is what causes the sensation of movement.

Clock

Unfortunately, after what we've just seen, our problems are not over. How often the function is run depends on the device and parallel tasks that are running. It will usually be 60 times per second, but this is not guaranteed and can decrease. This will mean that the animation will run very slowly or very quickly, which for our purposes is not acceptable. For example, walking or running animation needs to be executed certain time to look realistic.

Three.js incorporates the class ***THREE.Clock***, with the method ***getDelta(),*** which allows us to calculate the seconds that have passed from one run to another. Thus, if we want to rotate an object 2 units per second, we multiply *2*delta,* where delta is the result of the method ***getDelta().***

```
...
clock = new THREE.Clock();
...
function animate() {
```

```
        requestAnimationFrame( animate );

        var delta = clock.getDelta();
        mesh.rotation.x += delta * 0.5;
        mesh.rotation.y += delta * 2;
        mesh.position.x += dir*delta;
        if (mesh.position.x > 2) {
            dir=-1;
        } else if (mesh.position.x < - 2)  {
            dir=1;
        }
        renderer.render( scene, camera );
}
```

C2 - TREEJS: PREPARING THE DEVELOPMENT ENVIRONMENT

When we develop solutions with *Three.js* the simplest way to test results is to open the local file with the browser. Unfortunately, this solution will not work in all cases, and will generate a security error when loading textures with images and models.

It's best to work with a web server installed locally, because it will generate an experience as close as to that of the end user. Now we will see several suggestions to run our creations smoothly.

SOLVING THE "CROSS-ORIGIN-DOMAIN" ERROR

This security flaw is easily reproducible if you open the following link https://www.thefiveplanets.org/b01/c02/01-solve-cross-origin-issues.html.

When run, it will produce an error like the one shown in Figure *2.1*. The informational message will contain references to the crossed origins error (*cross-origin*) or security error (*security-error*) depending on the browser we use.

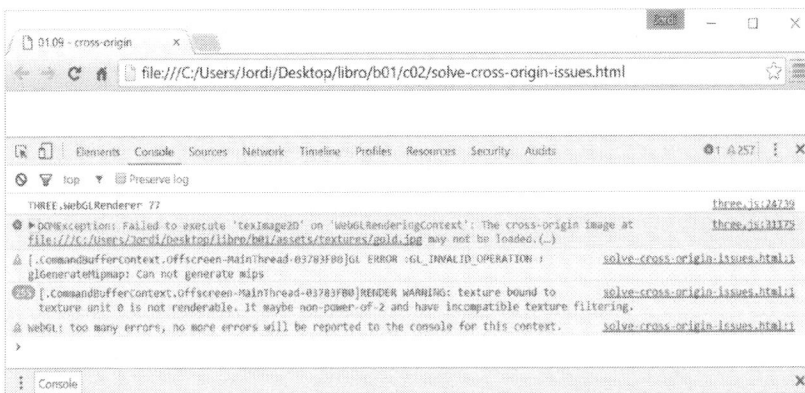

Fig. 2.1 Error shown in Chrome

The browser gives us this message and stops the execution of *JavaScript* to prevent access to personal data and thus prevent attacks on our device. When we are developing and we know that the source files are safe, it's useful for us to disable this security check.

With *Chrome* and *Firefox,* we can easily configure the browser to allow access to files from *Ajax calls*. Remember that these steps are not necessary if you run a local web server.

Chrome

To open *Chrome* and deactivate the security check we must specify the following parameter "*--allow-file-access-from-files*" as we run it.

The command will be different depending on the operating system that we use:

For Windows run the following command:

```
chrome.exe --allow-file-access-from-files
```

You can also create a ".*bat*" file; for example, "*runchrome.bat*" with the following contents:

```
Start "Chrome" "chrome.exe" --allow-file-access-from-files
Exit
```

For Linux, the command is as follows:

```
google-chrome --allow-file-access-from-files
```

For Mac, the order to write is:

```
open -a Google\chrome --args --allow-file-access-from-files
```

Remember that you can only use the parameter if Chrome is not running at that time, so we must close any instance of the program beforehand. Once you finish running the test close *Google Chrome*, because if you do not do this them the system is more vulnerable to attack.

Firefox

For Firefox, you need to open the browser and perform the following steps:

1. Enter the URL *about:config*. After this, a warning message indicating that the changes you make can have a negative impact on computer security and performance of the application will appear. Press the button to continue.

2. Find *security.fileuri.strict_origin_policy* and change its value to false.

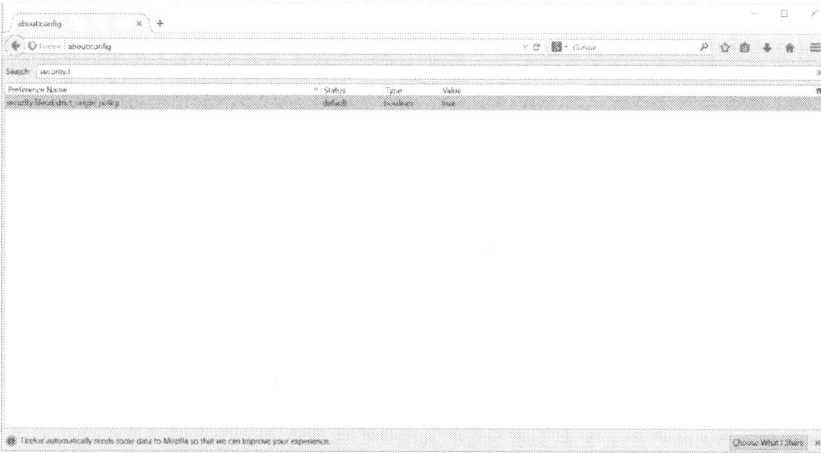

Fig. 2.2 Configuration Screen for FireFox.

3. Now you can open the link without problems, but remember that you have to disable the option to maintain secure navigation.

Once the problem is solved, you should see the next image when opening the link locally.

Fig. 2.3 Screen with texture loaded, once the security error is fixed.

INSTALLING A LOCAL WEB SERVER

In order to test web pages locally, and get a closer look at what o the end user will experience, you should definitely use a web server. To do this you will see some options that I've divided into two options.

One is offered by portable servers that do not require installation. It's sufficient to just run them in order to be able to create a server that is ready to use. They are a very attractive option because we can run them directly from a USB.

The second option is to install a server on your computer permanently so you can safely try out your creations. This option gives us more functionality and options of parameterization. However, for unfamiliar users, configuring and installing a server is usually time-consuming and extremely complex.

Portable servers

PWS (Apache + MySQL + PHP)

PWS is a lightweight, portable web server for *Windows*, which stands out for its direct interface where, we can modify the settings and activate or deactivate modules *Apache* or *PHP* with just a few clicks.

It also includes reference files with documentation on technologies such as *CSS3, JQuery, MySQL, PHP* or *Apache.*

You can download it here: http://sourceforge.net/projects/portableserver/

UwAmp (Apache + MySQL + PHP)

UwAmp is a server for Windows with a very convenient, useful interface. Besides the usual options, it features a *CPU* usage statistics graph for each server, customised configuration managers for *Apache*, *MySQL* and *PHP*, a *SQLite* database administrator and frequently used applications such as *PHPMyAdmin* or *XDebug*. It also supports multiple different versions of *PHP*.

You can download it here: http://www.uwamp.com

Mongose

Mongose is a portable server and has been available since 2004. Like the previous servers, you can open it from the folder where the code is, by copying the executable file. In this way, you have a server without needing to install or configure it. You can download the server from the following links:

https://github.com/cesanta/mongoose
https://www.cesanta.com/products/binary

Non-portable servers.

XAMPP

Perhaps one of the best known non-portable servers is *XAMPP*. It incorporates an *Apache* server, a management system for *MySQL* databases and languages like *PHP* and *Perl*. It also offers support for managing *FTP* accounts, access to databases through *PHPMyAdmin*, *SQLite* databases and other features.

It also includes a *Mercury* mail server for sending emails, a *Tomcat* server for *JSP servers* and an *FTP FileZilla* server.

It's cross-platform, so it works on Windows, Linux, Mac and even Solaris systems.

You can download the server here:

https://www.apachefriends.org

MAMP

Like the previous servers, *MAMP* incorporates *Apache*, *MySQL*, *PHP*, *perl*, and *Python*. Its main advantage is that it's easy to install and remove. *WAMP* is offered under *GNU* General Public License *(GNU GPL)*. Therefore, it can be freely distributed within the limits of this license.

There is a version for *Windows* and *Mac*. You can download it from the following link:

http://www.mamp.info

Web server for Node.js

The last proposal that we'll look at is through *Node.js*. If you have *Node.js* on your computer, you can use the command *"npm"* to install a simple web server.

To configure a local web server for *Node.js* you just need to follow the steps listed below:

First you must install *node.js* from https://nodejs.org , if you do not already have it. You can check if it's already installed on your computer by running the command **npm** from the command line (system symbol in *Windows*). The output it produces is similar to the following piece of text:

```
Usage: npm <command>

where <command> is one of:
add-user, adduser, apihelp, ...
```

Now we can install the server with the following command. We need to be connected to the internet to do this.

```
npm install -g http-server
```

Once completed, we are ready to start the web server using the following command line:

```
http-server
```

When we run the instruction, the following text will appear:

```
Starting up http-server, serving ./
Available on:
http://127.0.0.1:8080
Hit CTRL-C to stop the server
```

Now any file in the folder from where we ran the command is accessible through the URL http://127.0.0.1:8080. We can close the server by pressing *CTRL-C*.

STATISTICS (STATS.JS)

When we are creating complex applications with *Three.js*, especially games with many objects and animations, we must make sure that we do not exceed the limitations of the system. To do this you can download the library *stats.js* https://github.com/mrdoob/stats.js/ that allows you to monitor bottlenecks, generating statistics of:

- **FPS** *Frames* rendered per second. This value should never be lower than 30. It's recommended that this value is close to 60.
- **MS** Milliseconds required to render a *frame*. The lower the number the better.
- **MB** Megabytes of memory reserved. (Run *Chrome* with the parameter **--enable-required-memory-info** in order to obtain these statistics)

The library even allows us to define our own statistics and is perfectly integrated with *Three.js*, because its creator is the same person who originally started the *Three.js* project.

To use the library simply include it with the following instruction: <script src="//rawgit.com/mrdoob/stats.js/master/build/stats.min.js"></script>. If you have downloaded it replace the URL with the correct direction. You can see an example of its use:

https://www.thefiveplanets.org/b01/c02/02-statistics.html.

In the example, we've defined a function "*createStats*," which creates a box with statistics on the top left hand corner of the screen.

```
function createStats() {
    var stats = new Stats();
    stats.setMode(0); // 0: fps, 1: ms, 2: mb, 3+: custom

    return stats;
}
```

With *stats.setMode* we specify the type of statistics to show by default (0 - Frames rendered per second, 1 - Milliseconds required to render a frame, and 2 - Megabytes of memory used). The function is run from the method "*Init*", where we assign the object to a global variable *stats*, so that it can be referenced from other parts of JavaScript.

```
stats = createStats();
```

Every time we come back to paint the scene we must force an update of statistics by calling the *update* function.

```
function render() {
    renderer.render(scene, camera);

    ....

    requestAnimationFrame(render);

    stats.update();
}
```

In Figure *2.4* we see the statistics box that appears when you run the example. We can alternate between statistics by *clicking* on the box.

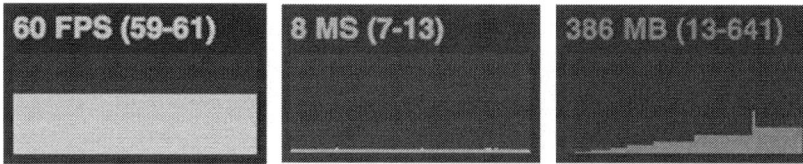

Fig. 2.4 Table with statistics.

UI CONTROL

When we are developing, it's often necessary to adjust the values of certain variables for optimal viewing. We may want to change the scale, orientation, or colour of an object to view it better or if we simply want to experiment with the properties offered by *Threee.js*. All we need to do is edit the values of the variables in the source code and reload the HTML files. This process can be tedious and time consuming.

Therefore, we can use the library *dat-gui* to create a graphical interface that allows us to modify the variables used to draw the *Three.js* scene quickly. You can download the latest version of the library from:

https://github.com/dataarts/dat.gui

In the following link, we see a basic example of a box that we've added, in the top right hand corner, which has three variables that can be altered to change the behaviour of the scene (the opacity and colour of the cube, and the rotation speed of the camera):

https://www.thefiveplanets.org/b01/c02/03-controls.html.

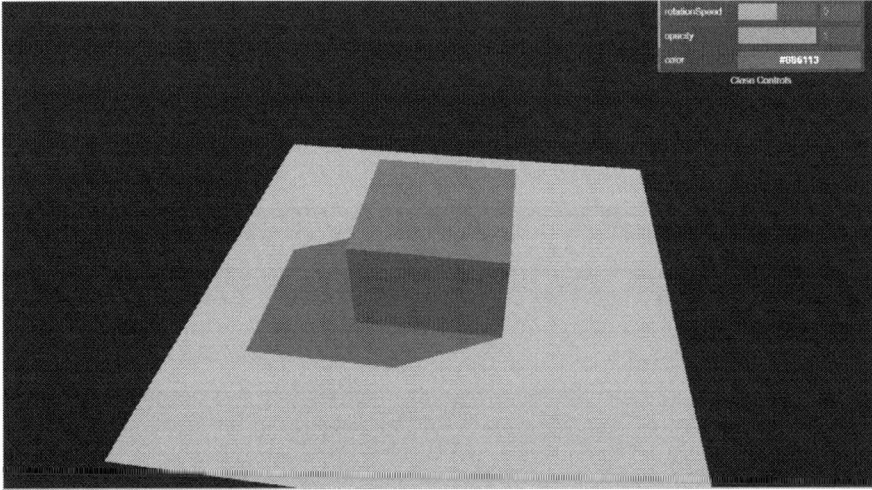

Fig. 2.5 Example of incorporating a User Interface created with dat-gui.

If we look at the example, we firstly see that we've included the reference to the JavaScript downloaded by the browser in the upper part:

```
<script src="dat.gui.min.js"></script>
```

Secondly, we've created an object which contains the variables that we wish to monitor and their initial values. We've assigned the object to a global variable to be able to access it from anywhere in the JavaScript code.

```
var control;
function init() {

    ...
    control = new function() {
      this.rotationSpeed = 0.005;
      this.opacity = 0.6;
      this.color = 0x086113;
    };
    addControlGui(control);
}
```

Thirdly, we've defined the function *addControlGui*, where we generate the user interface and link each property with the appropriate field.

```
function addControlGui(controlObject) {
    var gui = new dat.GUI();
    gui.add(controlObject, 'rotationSpeed', -1, 1);
    gui.add(controlObject, 'opacity', 0.1, 1);
    gui.addColor(controlObject, 'color');
}
```

Note that we've specified four arguments when creating a new field (*gui.add*).

The first argument is the JavaScript object that contains the variables. In our case, it's the object which contains the variables. The second argument is the name of the variable to be added, which should point to one of the variables (or functions) available in the object that is provided in the first argument. The third argument is the minimum value to be displayed in the GUI. The last argument specifies the maximum value that should be shown.

Now that we have a graphical user interface that can be used to control variables, the only thing left to do in the rendering loop of the scene is to consult the values to update the scene.

```
function render() {
    var delta = clock.getDelta();
    var rotSpeed = delta*control.rotationSpeed;
    camera.position.x= camera.position.x * Math.cos(rotSpeed)
        + camera.position.z * Math.sin(rotSpeed);
    camera.position.z = camera.position.z * Math.cos(rotSpeed)
        - camera.position.x * Math.sin(rotSpeed);
    camera.lookAt(scene.position);
    var cube= scene.getObjectByName('cube').material
    cube.material.opacity = control.opacity;
    cube.material.color = new THREE.Color(control.color);
    requestAnimationFrame(render);
    renderer.render(scene, camera);
}
```

The graphic interface can be hidden or shown by pressing the *H* key.

Field types to use in the interface

We've only seen a small group of the available fields in the example. The library will be adapted to a controller type according to which type of variable is added or which various parameters are specified. We can see some examples below.

- To add a drop-down list field to choose a text:

```
gui.add (controlObject, 'message',
```

```
[ 'cube', 'sphere', 'plane' ] );
```

- To add a drop-down list field to select values:

```
gui.add(controlObject,'speed',
{ Stopped: 0, Slow: 0.1, Fast: 5 } );
```

- To specify minimum and maximum numbers or the increment value:

```
// Increase
gui.add(controlObject, 'noiseStrength').step(5);
// Minimum and maximum
gui.add(controlObject, 'growthSpeed', -5, 5);
// Minimum and increment
gui.add(controlObject, 'maxSize').min(0).step(0.25);
```

- To create a button with an executable script:

```
controlObject.showmessage=function () { alert('message')}
// Min and max
gui.add(controlObject, 'growthSpeed', -5, 5);
```

- We can use the function *addColor* to create a colour box. Note that in the example, the performance of the function changes according to the type of variable we specify, since the colour can be represented in various ways (such as a *string*, an *array of* 3 or 4 numbers or as an object).

```
var controlObject = new function() {
    // CSS string
    this.color0 = "#ffae23";
    // RGB array
    this.color1 = [ 0, 128, 255 ];
    // RGB with opacity
    this.color2 = [ 0, 128, 255, 0.3 ];
    // Hue, saturation, value
    this.color3 = { h: 350, s: 0.9, v: 0.3 };
};
var gui = new dat.GUI();

gui.addColor(text, 'color0');
gui.addColor(text, 'color1');
gui.addColor(text, 'color2');
gui.addColor(text, 'color3');
```

Fig.2.6 Example of colour selector.

- For a checkbox, it is enough to pass as a parameter a variable of type Boolean.

```
controlObject.visible=true;
gui.add(controlObject, 'visible');
```

Folders

To make it easy to access to the properties we can add them in folders that can be folded or unfolded as shown in Figure 2.7.

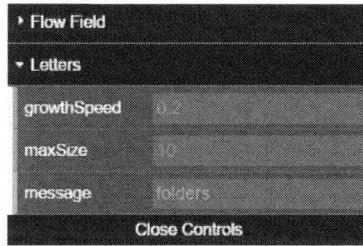

Fig.2.7 Ejemplo de carpetas anidadas.

```
var gui = new dat.GUI();

var f1 = gui.addFolder('Flow Field');
f1.add(controlObject, 'speed');

var f2 = gui.addFolder('Letters');
f2.add(controlObject,'growthSpeed');
f2.add(controlObject,'maxSize');
f2.add(controlObject,'message');
f2.open();
```

Events

In addition to what we've seen, we can add events that trigger at the time of changing the value of a variable. Here's an example below:

```
var controller = gui.add(controlObject, 'maxSize', 0, 10);

controller.onChange( function(value) {
```

```
/* It is fired at every change of value, Keystroke, etc..*/
});

controller.onFinishChange( function(value) {
/* It shoots when you lose focus.*/
alert("El valor es " + value);
});
```

DETECTING WEBGL SUPPORT

Most modern browsers support *WebGL,* but older versions and some devices do not support it. It's therefore a good idea to make sure the browser you are using supports *WebGL* when creating an instance of *THREE.WebGLRender.* If it's not supported, the gaming experience may be diminished as JavaScript errors and a blank screen can appear during gameplay. One way to check for *WebGL* is by using the function attached below.

You can see an example of how it works in the following link:
https://www.thefiveplanets.org/b01/c02/04-detect-webgl-support.html.

```
function detectWebGL() {
    var testCanvas = document.createElement("canvas");
    var gl = null;
    try {
        gl = testCanvas.getContext("webgl",{antialias: false, depth: false });
    } catch (x) {
        gl = null;
    }
    if (gl==null) {
        try {
            gl = testCanvas.getContext("experimental-webgl", {antialias: false, depth: false });
        } catch (x) {
            gl = null;
        }
    }
    if (gl) {
        return true;
    } else {
        return false;
    }
}
```

C3 - THREEJS: GEOMETRIES, MATERIALS, LIGHTS AND SHADOWS

GEOMETRIES

As we've seen, objects are defined indicating their vertices (*THREE.Vector3*) and faces (triangles) (*THREE.Face3*). Luckily there are several predefined figures in *Three.js* that make this task easier.

Predefined 3D geometries

You can see an example with some *3D* geometries that *Three.js* offers on the following webpage.
https://www.thefiveplanets.org/b01/c03/01-geometrias3D.html.

Below I detail the most relevant geometries and their parameters.

Cube (THREE.BoxGeometry)

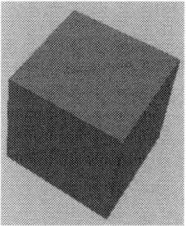

BoxGeometry lets you create a cube with its width, height and depth specified. You can use the number of segments to divide the faces into small rectangles. In the accompanying example, we've highlighted its faces.

THREE.CubeGeometry(Width, Height, Depth, Segments Width, Segments Height, Segments Depth);

Example:
var cube=new THREE.CubeGeometry(4, 4, 4, 1, 1, 1);

Sphere (THREE.Sphere)

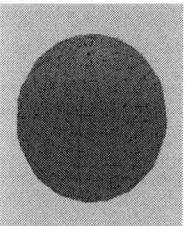

To create a sphere, specify its radius and the segments in which it's divided both horizontally and vertically; the more segments we specify the more it will resemble a real sphere, but this will consume more memory and *CPU* resources it.

THREE.SphereGeometry (Radius, SegmentsHorizontal, SegmentsVertical);

Example:
var sphere=new THREE.SphereGeometry (2, 16, 16);

Polyhedron (THREE. IcosahedronGeometry, THREE.DodecahedronGeometry, THREE.OctahedronGeometry, THREE.TetrahedronGeometry)

A polyhedron is, in the sense given to the term in geometry, a body whose faces are flat and which encloses a finite volume. Below I list those that *Three.js* provides us.

ICOSAHEDRON

This is a polyhedron with 20 faces. To create it we use the following parameters: the radius and the detail. This last parameter indicates how many times a face will be split.

THREE.IcosahedronGeometry (Radius, Detail);

Example:
var icosahedron=new THREE.IcosahedronGeometry (2, 0);

DODECAHEDRON

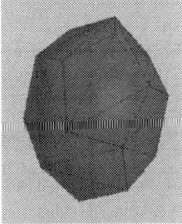

This is a polyhedron with 12 evenly distributed faces. To create it we specify the radius and the number of times the faces will be divided (detail).

THREE.DodecahedronGeometry (Radius, Detail);

Example:
var dodecahedron=new THREE.DodecahedronGeometry (2, 0);

OCTAHEDRON

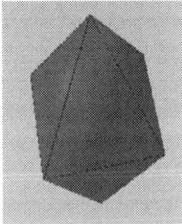

This is a polyhedron with 8 evenly distributed faces. To create it we specify the radius and the number of times the faces will be divided (detail).

THREE.OctahedronGeometry (Radius, Detail);

Example:
var octahedron=new THREE.OctahedronGeometry (2, 0);

TETRAHEDRON

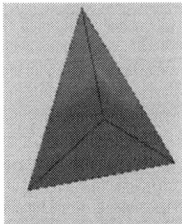

This is a polyhedron with 4 evenly distributed faces. To create it we specify the radius and the number of times the faces will be divided (detail).

THREE.TetrahedronGeometry (Radius, Detail);

Example:
var tetrahedron=new THREE.TetrahedronGeometry (2, 0);

Cylinder (THREE.CylinderGeometry)

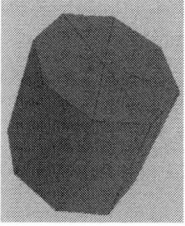

The cylinder is a columnar shape. To create it we specify the radius of the top circle, the radius of the lower circle, the column height, the segments in which the circles are divided (8 by default), the segments in which the face is divided, which join the upper and lower circles, and finally if it's an open or closed cylinder.

THREE.CylinderGeometry (Superior radius, Inferior radius, Height, Segments circle, Segments Column, isOpen);

Example:
var cylinder=new THREE.CylinderGeometry (2, 2, 4);

Cone (THREE.ConeGeometry)

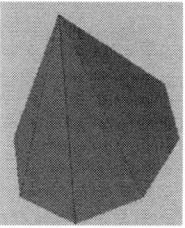

In geometry, a right cone is a solid of revolution generated by the rotation of a right-angle triangle around one of its legs. To create it we specify the circle radius of the base, the cone height, the number of circle segments and if it's an open or closed cone (with or without a circle in the base).

THREE.ConeGeometry (Radius, Height, Segments, IsOpen);

Example:
var cone=new THREE.ConeGeometry (2, 4, 8);

Torus (THREE.TorusGeometry)

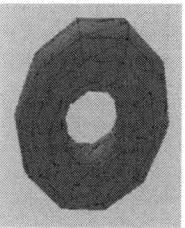

This is a donut-shaped figure. As parameters, we specify the radius of the outer circle, the width of the tube, segments into which the tube surface is divided and finally the segments into which the *torus* is divided.

THREE.TorusGeometry (Radius, WidthTube, SegmentsRadius, SegmentsTorus);

Example:
var torus=new THREE.TorusGeometry (2, 1, 10, 10);

TorusKnot (THREE.TorusKnotGeometry)

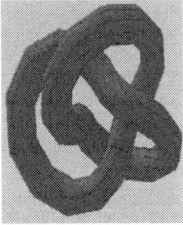

This corresponds to the figure of a knot. As parameters, we specify the radius, the width of the tube, segments into which the tube surface is divided and the segments making up the knot.

THREE.TorusKnotGeometry ();

Example:
var torusknot=new THREE.TorusKnotGeometry (2, 0.5, 35, 10);

Predefined 2D geometries

You can see some of plane figures offered by *Three.js* on the following webpage.

https://www.thefiveplanets.org/b01/c03/02-geometrias2D.html.

Plane (THREE.Plane)

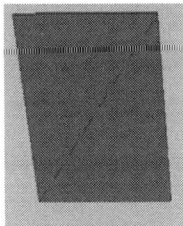

This corresponds to a rectangle. To create it we specify the width, the height, the segments into which the width is divided and the segments into which the height is divided. By default, the last two parameters are 1.

THREE.PlaneGeometry (Width, Height, SegmentsWidth, SegmentsHeight);

Example:
var plane=new THREE.PlaneGeometry (4, 4);

Circle and polygon (THREE.Circle)

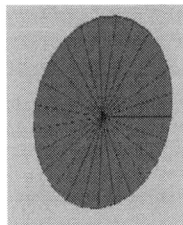

This corresponds to a regular polygon. The first parameter is the radius, the second is the number of sides. The more sides there are the more it will resemble a circle.

THREE.CircleGeometry (Radius, Number of sides);

Example:
var circle=new THREE.CircleGeometry (2, 25);

Ring (THREE.Ring)

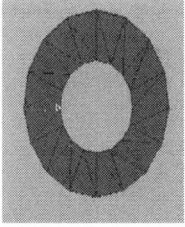

This is a circle with one hole. The first parameter is the radius of the hole, the second is the radius of the circle, and the last is the number of sides.

THREE.RingGeometry (holeRadius, Radius, Number of sides);

Example:
var ring=new THREE. RingGeometry (1, 2, 16);

Customised geometries

In the first chapter, we've seen that another way to create customised geometry is by providing the list of vertices (points), and their faces (triangles which join 3 points). You can remember this concept by running the example of the plane triangle we saw in the first chapter here:

https://www.thefiveplanets.org/b01/c01/04-geometry.html.

Next, we'll learn how to create plane geometries using the class ***THREE.Shape*** and give them volume by using the class ***THREE.ExtrudeGeometry***.

Free 2D figure (THREE.Shape and THREE.ShapeGeometry)

THREE.Shape allows you to create plane figures using two methods. The first is by indicating an array of points (*x, y*) so that a line is plotted from point to point following the order of the array. In the second method, we have an imaginary pointer that we can move and draw straight lines, arcs etc. with to form the flat shape.

The following code creates a yellow star using the array of points. You can see the code here: https://www.thefiveplanets.org/b01/c03/03-start.html

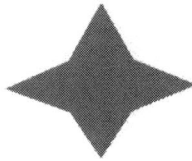

Fig.3.14 Example of THREE.Shape.

```
var startShape = new THREE.Shape([
    new THREE.Vector2(0,3),
    new THREE.Vector2(1,1),
    new THREE.Vector2(3,0),
    new THREE.Vector2(1,-1),
    new THREE.Vector2(0,-3),
```

```
    new THREE.Vector2(-1,-1),
    new THREE.Vector2(-3,0),
    new THREE.Vector2(-1,1)
]);
var startGeometry = new THREE.ShapeGeometry( startShape );
var startMaterial = new THREE.MeshLambertMaterial(
    {color: 0x827a06,
    transparent:true,
    opacity:1,
    side: THREE.DoubleSide });
var start = new THREE.Mesh(startGeometry, startMaterial);
start.name='start';
start.position.set(0,1,0);
```

We can use the same example, but instead of indicating the points, we can draw using the imaginary pointer. In this case, we use the function ***moveTo*** to specify the point where to begin drawing the star and the instruction ***lineTo*** to draw lines between the vertices. You can see the code at:

https://www.thefiveplanets.org/b01/c03/04-start1.html

```
var startShape = new THREE.Shape();
startShape.moveTo(0,3);
startShape.lineTo(1,1);
startShape.lineTo(3,0);
startShape.lineTo(1,-1);
startShape.lineTo(0,-3);
startShape.lineTo(-1,-1);
startShape.lineTo(-3,0);
startShape.lineTo(-1,1);
```

Other functions you can use are ***arc and absarc*** to draw arcs; and ***bezierCurveTo*** and ***quadraticCurveTo*** to draw curves.

For more complex shapes we can use the property ***holes***, which allows you to create holes in its surface. The holes are flat figures created as we've seen, but instead of instantiating the class *THREE.Shape*, we use *THREE.Path*. In fact, the class *THREE.Shape* inherits from the class *THREE.Path*, so the methods *moveTo, lineTo, arc* and *bezierCurveTo* are available in both classes and we can even create a *Path* from an array of points in the same way.

For example, we can create a hole in the centre of the star by adding the following code:

```
var holePath = new THREE.Path()
holePath.moveTo( 0.5, 0 );
```

```
holePath.absarc( 0, 0, 0.5, 0, Math.PI*2, true );
startShape.holes.push( holePath );
```

You can see the code here: https://www.thefiveplanets.org/b01/c03/05-start2.html

Fig. 3.15 Example of THREE.Shape with a hole.

Click on the following link to see more figures created directly using the class *THREE.Shape* https://www.thefiveplanets.org/b01/c03/06-shape.html.

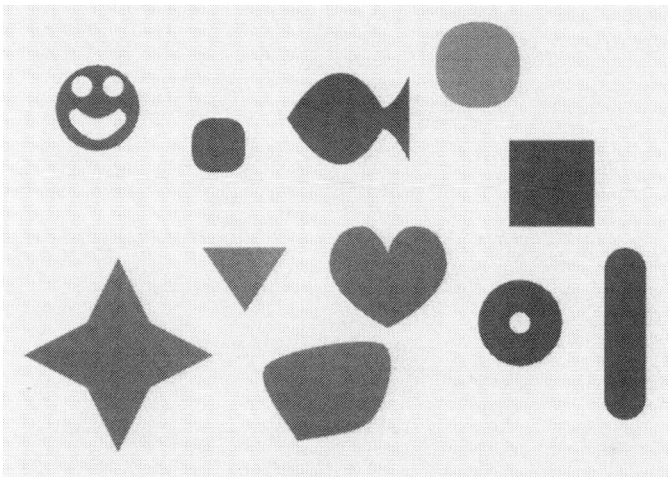

Fig. 3.16 Example of THREE.Shape with multiples figures.

Giving volume to a flat figure (THREE.ExtrudeGeometry)

We've seen how to create plane figures. Now we'll see how to give them volume. We'll continue using the example of the star with a hole in the centre and will give it volume by using **THREE.ExtrudeGeometry**.

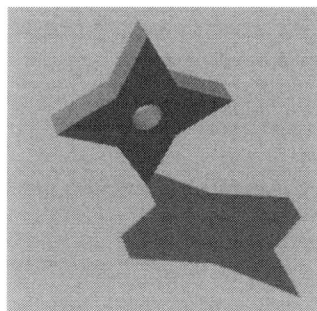

Fig. 3.17 Example of THREE.ExtrudeGeometry.

The only thing we've changed in the example is that we've used the class *THREE.ExtrudeGeometry* instead of using *THREE.ShapeGeometry* to create the geometry. As the first parameter, we specify the plane figure and secondly the options for generating volume.

```
var startGeometry = new THREE.ExtrudeGeometry( startShape,
{amount: 1, bevelEnabled: false} );
```

Amount in this case is the most important property because it allows us to specify the thickness. Moreover we disable the option to create a bevel when we set **bevelEnabled** to *false*. In the next section, you can see some of these options explained in more detail.

Click on the following link to see the example of the full star: http://www.thefiveplanets.org/b01/c03/07-start3.html.

3D text (THREE.TextGeometry)

A very interesting feature of *Three.js* is that it allows you to create *3D* texts easily. For this we need a font with a format ready to use in *Three.js* (*typefaced*). We can convert any font to the format *typefaced* by clicking on the following link: http://gero3.github.io/facetype.js/. It's only necessary to create an instance of the class *THREE.TextGeometry*, indicating the text to be written and font characteristics (font name, font size, relief etc.) as parameters. You can see an example here: https://www.thefiveplanets.org/b01/c03/08-text3D.html.

Fig. 3.18 Example of THREE.Text3D.

```
var geometry = new THREE.TextGeometry( data.text, {
    font: font,
    size: data.size,
    height: data.height,
```

```
        curveSegments: data.curveSegments,
        bevelEnabled: data.bevelEnabled,
        bevelThickness: data.bevelThickness,
        bevelSize: data.bevelSize
} );
geometry.center();
```

Unfortunately, we must load the font on the memory before we're able to use *textGeometry*. There are two ways to do this depending on whether we've converted the font to a JSON or JavaScript format.

When using JSON we load it asynchronously as shown in the example and in this case, we wait for the operation to end in order to use it.

```
var material= new THREE.MeshPhongMaterial( {
        color: 0x156289,
        emissive: 0x072534,
        shading: THREE.FlatShading
} );
var mesh = new THREE.Mesh(new THREE.Geometry(),material ));
scene.add( mesh );

var loader = new THREE.FontLoader();
loader.load( '../data/fonts/gentilis_bold.typeface.json', function ( font ) {
        var geometry = new THREE.TextGeometry( "This is a TEXT", {
            font: "gentilis",
            weight: "bold",
            style:"normal",
            size: 5,
            height: 2,
            curveSegments: 12,
            bevelEnabled: false
        } );
        geometry.center();
        mesh.geometry.dispose();
        mesh.geometry=geometry;
} );
```

When using sources in JavaScript format, we can include them directly at the head of the page:

```
<script src="../data/fonts/gentilis_bold.typeface.js">
```

The different parameters to use are:

Parameter	Description
font	This is the name of the font to use.
size	We can set the font size with this parameter.
height	This defines the depth of the relief of the text.
curveSegments	If a letter has curves (e.g. the letter o), this parameter specifies the detail of the curve. The higher the value, the greater the quality of the letter, but this also consumes more resources.
bevelEnabled	If you enable this property (value *true*) a bevel will be created around the letter. When we use the property *bevelThickness* we specify the depth of the bevel, while with *bevelSize* we specific how far it expands sideways.

MATERIALS

As we've specified, the materials are "*the skin*" of the figures and serve to define what colour each side of a figure is. They also specify how light and shadows act on the surface. The materials are instances of *THREE.Material*.

As with the geometries, *Three.js* offers several classes to create different types of materials depending on the effect we want to project.

THREE.MeshBasicMaterial

This material is not affected by light and shadows, so it's visible without the need to add lights. It has a uniform solid colour or solid lines connecting vertices (*whireframe*) depending of the parameters. With this material, it's difficult to distinguish the volumes and distances, or even overlapping figures. It's only affected by fog (*fog*) should it be activated, which can make distinguishing its shape easier.

Fig. 3.19 Example of MeshBasicMaterial.

```
var geometry = new THREE.TorusKnotGeometry( 10, 3, 100, 16 );
var material = new THREE.MeshBasicMaterial({ color: 0x2194CE});
var mesh = new THREE.Mesh( geometry, material );
```

You can click on the following link to see an example:

https://www.thefiveplanets.org/b01/c03/09-mesh-basic-material.html.

THREE.MeshNomalMaterial

This material, like the previous one, is not affected by light and shadows, so it's visible without the need to add lights.

The object surface colour varies between red, green and blue hues, depending on the magnitude of the values *X/Y/ Z* of the normal vector (the normal vector is a vector perpendicular to the surface).

It's a material that allows volumes to be easily distinguished, without being affected by light, so it's useful for illustrating examples.

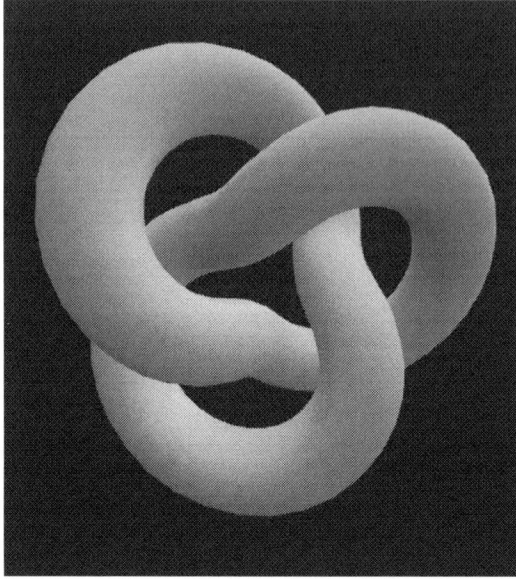

Fig. 3.20 Example of MeshNormalMaterial..

```
var geometry = new THREE.ToruoKnotGcometi y( 10, 3, 100, 18 );
var material = new THREE.MeshNormalMaterial();
var mesh = new THREE.Mesh( geometry, material );
```

In the following link, you can see a complete example:

https://www.thefiveplanets.org/b01/c03/10-mesh-normal-material.html.

THREE.MeshDepthMaterial

Like the previous two materials, it's not affected by light either. The surface has a grey colour that lightens or darkens according to the distance from the camera. It's often used when designing scenes, before applying more elaborate textures.

Fig. 3.21 Example of MeshDepthMaterial.

```
var geometry = new THREE.TorusKnotGeometry( 10, 3, 100, 16 );
var material = new THREE.MeshDepthMaterial({ color: 0x2194CE});
var mesh = new THREE.Mesh( geometry, material );
```

In the following link, you can see a complete example:

https://www.thefiveplanets.org/b01/c03/11-mesh-depth-material.html.

THREE.MeshLambertMaterial

Lights affect the surface of the object, so that it darkens or lightens depending on the distance from the light, but it does not generate glare. In order to visualise it, there needs to be some light shining on the surface, otherwise it will appear black.

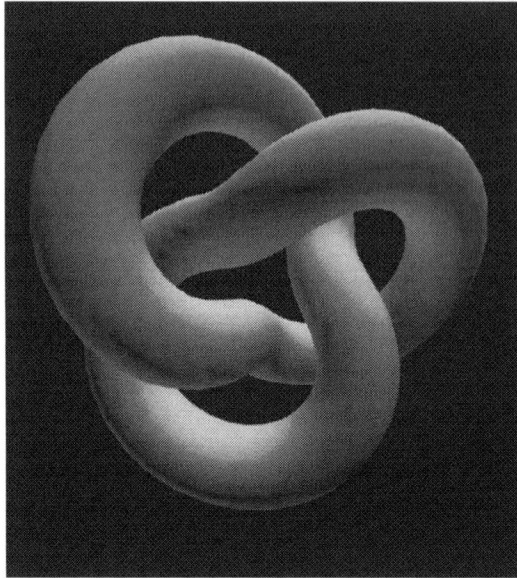

Fig. 3.22 Example of MeshLambertMaterial.

```
var geometry = new THREE.TorusKnotGeometry( 10, 3, 100, 16 );
var material = new THREE.MeshLambertMaterial({ color: 0x2194CE});
var mesh = new THREE.Mesh( geometry, material );
```

In the following link, you can see a complete example:

https://www.thefiveplanets.org/b01/c03/12-mesh-lambert-material.html.

THREE.MeshPhongMaterial

This material is the most used for the final representation of the scenes, as it's affected by light, darkens because of shadows and creates glare. For example, a white light shining directly on the object will produce reflections, while parts less exposed to light will darken. In order to display the figure there must be some light, otherwise it will appear black.

Fig. 3.23 Example of MeshPhongMaterial.

```
var geometry = new THREE.TorusKnotGeometry( 10, 3, 100, 16 );
var material = new THREE.MeshPhongMaterial({ color: 0x2194CE});
var mesh = new THREE.Mesh( geometry, material );
```

Click on the following link to see a complete example of this material:

https://www.thefiveplanets.org/b01/c03/13-mesh-phong-material.html.

THREE.MultiMaterial

This material is in fact an *array* of other primary materials, so that we can specify the chosen material for each surface. If you look at the example attached below you will see that we first create the *THREE.MultiMaterial* from an array of 10 items, then we assign each face of the figure one of 10 random materials (**geometry.faces[i].materialIndex**).

You can see a complete example of this here:

https://www.thefiveplanets.org/b01/c03/14-multi-material.html.

Fig. 3.24 Example of MeshMultiMaterial.

```
var geometry = new THREE.TorusKnotGeometry( 10, 3, 100, 16 );
var materials=[];

materials.push( new THREE.MeshLambertMaterial(
    { color: 0xdddddd,
     shading: THREE.FlatShading } ) );
materials.push( new THREE.MeshPhongMaterial(
    { color: 0xdddddd,
     specular: 0x009900,
     shininess: 30,
     shading: THREE.FlatShading } ) );
materials.push( new THREE.MeshNormalMaterial( ) );
materials.push( new THREE.MeshBasicMaterial(
    { color: 0xffaa00,
     transparent: true,
     blending: THREE.AdditiveBlending } ) );
materials.push( new THREE.MeshLambertMaterial(
    { color: 0xdddddd,
     shading: THREE.SmoothShading } ) );
materials.push( new THREE.MeshNormalMaterial(
    { shading: THREE.SmoothShading } ) );
materials.push( new THREE.MeshBasicMaterial(
    { color: 0xffaa00,
     wireframe: true } ) );
materials.push( new THREE.MeshDepthMaterial() );
materials.push( new THREE.MeshLambertMaterial(
    { color: 0x666666,
```

```
      emissive: 0xff0000,
      shading: THREE.SmoothShading } ) );
materials.push( new THREE.MeshPhongMaterial(
      { color: 0x000000,
      specular: 0x666666,
      emissive: 0xff0000,
      shininess: 10,
      shading: THREE.SmoothShading,
      opacity: 0.9,
      transparent: true } ) );

var material = new THREE.MultiMaterial( materials );

for ( var i = 0, l = geometry.faces.length; i < l; i ++ ) {
      var face = geometry.faces[ i ];
      face.materialIndex = Math.floor(
        Math.random() * materials.length );
}

geometry.sortFacesByMaterialIndex();
var mesh = new THREE.Mesh( geometry, material );
```

TEXTURES

We've seen how to alter the colours of objects, but this is not enough. It's very difficult to create realistic images merely by playing with solid colours, shadows and lights. Therefore, we need to use textures for objects that have many details.

Texture maps (or simply textures) are bitmap images displayed on the entire surface of the geometric shape. Image formats that can be used are web standards such as *JPEG* and *PNG*. We not only can create textures from image files, but can also create them using the image produced by the element *CANVAS HTML*. This allows us to draw on the surface of the object using the *APIs* of the *2D* drawing of the *CANVAS*. The textures can even be created from video elements, allowing video playback on the surface of an object.

We'll look at these dynamic capabilities for texturing in other books in the collection.

Here you can see the rotating cube we used above, but instead of a solid colour it has a texture.

Fig. 3.25. Example of a cube with a texture.

So, we've replaced the line:

```
var cubeMaterial = new THREE.MeshPhongMaterial( { color: 0x90abed, transparent: true, opacity:1});
```

with the following lines:

```
var textureLoader= new THREE.TextureLoader();
var texture=textureLoader.load("../data/graphics/logo.jpg");
var cubeMaterial = new THREE.MeshPhongMaterial({color: 0x90abed, map: texture, transparent: true,
opacity: 1});
```

You can see the example in the following link:

https://www.thefiveplanets.org/b01/c03/15-basic-texture.html.

Note that the image that we used in the example is not square, but it automatically changes shape to fit each face. *Three.js* allows you to specify several options of how to modify the image.

Remember that the example will not work if you run it from a local file. In Chapter Two of this book we've seen several solutions to this problem, from setting up a local web server to configuring the main browsers to allow us to load images locally from Ajax calls.

Multiple textures - UV Mapping

The example above may not be enough. For instance, what if we want different textures for different parts of the object? Fortunately, *Three.js* provides a couple of methods to do this. The first method is to use the class **THREE.MultiMaterial**, which we've already seen, or **THREE.MeshFaceMaterial.** Both work similarly, we have to provide a list of materials with different textures when using both of them.

For example, to convert the cube of the example to a dice, we have created several images with a different number of black tops for each face (from 1 to 6).

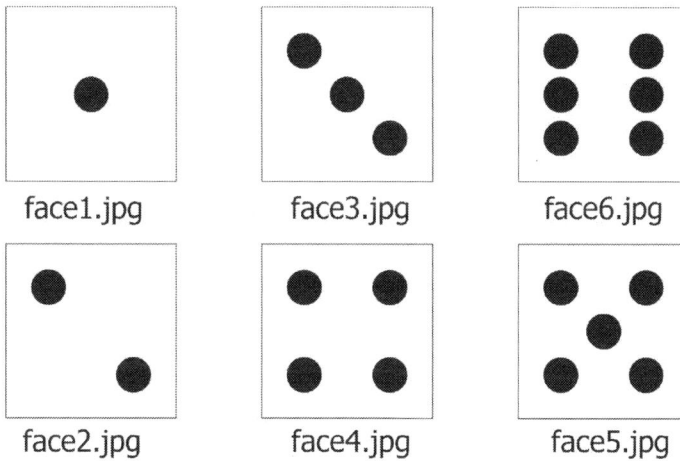

face1.jpg   face3.jpg   face6.jpg

face2.jpg   face4.jpg   face5.jpg

Fig. 3.26. Images of the die by the name of each file.

In the code, you only need to create an *array* with 6 different materials, each with 6 textures, and then create a multiple material.

```
var materials=[];
var dir="../data/graphics/textures/dice/";
materials.push (new THREE.MeshPhongMaterial(
    {color: 0x90abed,
     map:textureLoader.load( dir+"face1.jpg"),
     transparent:true, opacity:1}) );
materials.push (new THREE.MeshPhongMaterial(
    {color: 0x90abed,
     map:textureLoader.load( dir+"face2.jpg"),
     transparent:true, opacity:1}) );
materials.push( new THREE.MeshPhongMaterial(
    {color: 0x90abed,
     map:textureLoader.load( dir+"face3.jpg"),
     transparent:true, opacity:1}) );
materials.push( new THREE.MeshPhongMaterial(
    {color: 0x90abed,
     map:textureLoader.load(dir+"face4.jpg"),
     transparent:true, opacity:1}) );
materials.push( new THREE.MeshPhongMaterial(
    {color: 0x90abed
     map:textureLoader.load(dir+"face5.jpg"),
```

```
    transparent:true, opacity:1}) );
materials.push( new THREE.MeshPhongMaterial(
    {color: 0x90abed,
    map:textureLoader.load(dir+"face6.jpg"),
    transparent:true, opacity:1}) );
var cubeMaterial = new THREE.MeshFaceMaterial(materials);
var cube = new THREE.Mesh( cubeGeometry , cubeMaterial);
```

In addition, for easy viewing we've changed the position of the cube so that it floats in the air and turns on itself.

Fig. 3.27. Dice with 6 faces.

You can download the code example here:

https://www.thefiveplanets.org/b01/c03/16-multi-texture.html.

Creating and uploading an image for each side of our model becomes impractical when there are more faces. This also hinders performance and uses up resources. This leads us to the second method, which only uses one image and specifies which part of the image is displayed for each side of our 3D object (***UV Mapping***).

The first step is to join the 6 images on just one, as shown below.

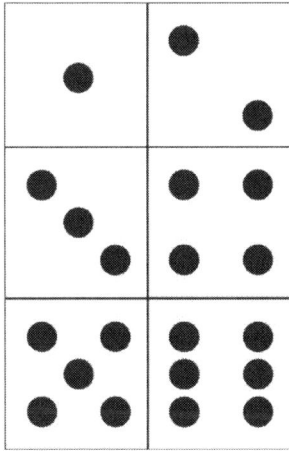

Fig. 3.28. Single image with the 6 faces of the cube.

With this we can replace the multiple material with a material with a single texture image. (See *Fig. 3.28.*).

```
var cubeMaterial = new THREE.MeshFaceMaterial (new THREE.MeshPhongMaterial({ color: 0x90abed,
map:textureLoader.load("../data/graphics/textures/dice/dice-texture.jpg"), transparent:true, opacity:1}));
```

As you can see, with this instruction we've gone back to the first example in this section, creating a single material with a single texture. The next step is to assign the various parts of our image to the individual faces of our cube.

With the following lines of code, we specify which part of the image corresponds to each face of the cube.

```
var face1 = [
    new THREE.Vector2(0, .666),
    new THREE.Vector2(.5, .666),
    new THREE.Vector2(.5, 1),
    new THREE.Vector2(0, 1)];
var face2 = [
    new THREE.Vector2(.5, .666),
    new THREE.Vector2(1, .666),
    new THREE.Vector2(1, 1),
    new THREE.Vector2(.5, 1)];
var face3 = [
    new THREE.Vector2(0, .333),
    new THREE.Vector2(.5, .333),
    new THREE.Vector2(.5, .666),
    new THREE.Vector2(0, .666)];
var face4 = [
    new THREE.Vector2(.5, .333),
    new THREE.Vector2(1, .333),
```

```
    new THREE.Vector2(1, .666),
    new THREE.Vector2(.5, .666)];
var face5 = [
    new THREE.Vector2(0, 0),
    new THREE.Vector2(.5, 0),
    new THREE.Vector2(.5, .333),
    new THREE.Vector2(0, .333)];
var face6 = [
    new THREE.Vector2(.5, 0),
    new THREE.Vector2(1, 0),
    new THREE.Vector2(1, .333),
    new THREE.Vector2(.5, .333)];
```

We create six *arrays*, one for each section of the image, which represents a face of the cube. Each *array* contains 4 points that define the limits of the image of the face. The coordinate values range from *0* and *1* where (*0, 0*) is the lower left corner and (*1, 1*) is the upper right corner.

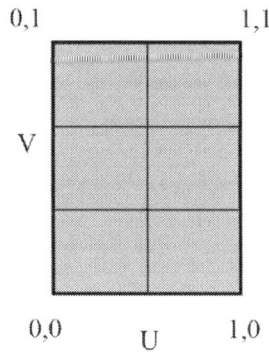

Fig. 3.29. Grid for the texture.

The coordinate system is expressed in terms of a percentage of the height and width of the image. To clarify this let us take a more detailed look at the matrix, which represents the face with a top (face1).

```
var face1 = [
    new THREE.Vector2(0, .666),
    new THREE.Vector2(.5, .666),
    new THREE.Vector2(.5, 1),
    new THREE.Vector2(0, 1)];
```

The picture represents the face of the cube with a mole, which is in the upper left corner of our texture. The coordinates start at the bottom left of the section of the image and continue in anti-clockwise direction.

The lower left corner is defined by:

0 - The left edge of the texture.

0.666 - Two-thirds from the bottom.

The lower right corner is defined by:

0.5 - Half the width.

0.666 - Two-thirds from the bottom.

The upper right corner is defined by:

0.5 - Half the width.

1 - The top edge of the texture.

The upper left corner is defined by:

0 - The left edge of the texture.

1 - The top edge of the texture.

Now that we've defined the images corresponding to each face of the cube in our texture, we can begin to apply them to the faces of our cube. The first thing we do is add the following line:

```
geometry.faceVertexUvs[0] = [];
```

This instruction clears the UV mapping that may exist in the cube. Then we add the following lines to assign each section of the face its corresponding image:

```
geometry.faceVertexUvs[0][0] = [ face1[0], face1[1], face1[3] ];
geometry.faceVertexUvs[0][1] = [ face1[1], face1[2], face1[3] ];

geometry.faceVertexUvs[0][2] = [ face2[0], face2[1], face2[3] ];
geometry.faceVertexUvs[0][3] = [ face2[1], face2[2], face2[3] ];

geometry.faceVertexUvs[0][4] = [ face3[0], face3[1], face3[3] ];
geometry.faceVertexUvs[0][5] = [ face3[1], face3[2], face3[3] ];

geometry.faceVertexUvs[0][6] = [ face4[0], face4[1], face4[3] ];
geometry.faceVertexUvs[0][7] = [ face4[1], face4[2], face4[3] ];

geometry.faceVertexUvs[0][8] = [ face5[0], face5[1], face5[3] ];
geometry.faceVertexUvs[0][9] = [ face5[1], face5[2], face5[3] ];

geometry.faceVertexUvs[0][10] = [ face6[0], face6[1], face6[3] ];
geometry.faceVertexUvs[0][11] = [ face6[1], face6[2], face6[3] ];
```

The property *faceVertexUvs* is an *array* of *arrays* containing mapping coordinates for each face of the geometric shape. Since the geometric shape is a cube in this case, the question of why there are 12 faces in the matrix arises. The reason is that each side of the cube is created from 2 triangles (as seen above), so that each triangle must be assigned individually. In previous examples, it was *Three.js* that was responsible for splitting the textures into triangles and assigning them to each face for us.

The order in which the coordinates are specified for each face is anti-clockwise.

The *arrays* to specify one of the 6 faces, which form the cube have been created in an anti-clockwise direction. If you look at the image below (*Fig. 3.30*) you'll see that we use the first triangle vertices at the indexes 0, 1 and 3, whilst we use the vertices at the indexes 1, 2 and 3 to map the upper triangle.

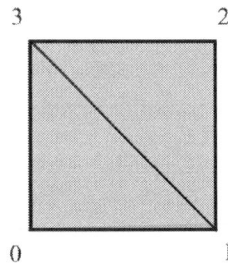

Fig. 3.30. Grid for a face of the cube.

You can see the complete example here:

https://www.thefiveplanets.org/b01/c03/17-uv-mapping.html.

In later chapters and other books in the series we'll discuss how to do mapping, without the need to execute it manually, by using external tools like *blender*.

Tip

The size of the textures can drastically reduce performance, so it's always advisable to minimize the size of images, which use, for example, JPG and reduce the quality of these images with programs like *Photoshop*.

Repeating texture

Often, we find that we need to repeat the same texture onto a surface.

For example, to represent a tile floor, we can repeat the image of one of the tiles or of a small group of them, rather than creating an image with all the tiles. *Three.js* allows you to customize the way in which the texture is repeated.

The first thing we need is an image in which we do not notice the connections between the two sides when it's repeated. As an example, we will create a brick wall and a parquet floor, and for this we will use two textures for each element.

Fig. 3.31. Floor texture.

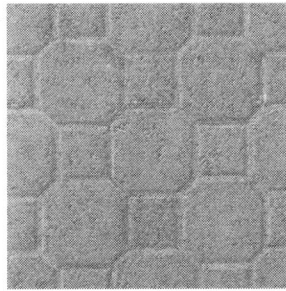

Fig. 3.32 Wall texture.

The first step is to load the two textures we are going to use.

```
var textureLoader = new THREE.TextureLoader();
var floorTexture = textureLoader.load("../data/graphics/textures/wall/floor.jpg");
....
var wallTexture = textureLoader.load("../data/graphics/textures/wall/wall.jpg");
```

Next, we specify the properties *wrapS* and *wrapT*:

```
wallTexture.wrapS=THREE.RepeatWrapping;
wallTexture.wrapT=THREE.RepeatWrapping;
floorTexture.wrapS=THREE.RepeatWrapping;
floorTexture.wrapT=THREE.RepeatWrapping;
```

These properties define whether we should stretch the texture sideways (*THREE.ClampToEdgeWrapping*) or repeat it (*THREE.RepeatWrapping*).

Now we create geometric shapes and assign textures:

```
var wallGeometry = new THREE.BoxGeometry(20, 6, 1);
var wallMaterial = new THREE.MeshPhongMaterial(
```

```
    {color: 0xffffff,
    map:wallTexture,
    transparent:true,
    opacity:1});
var wall = new THREE.Mesh(wallGeometry, wallMaterial);

var planeGeometry = new THREE.PlaneGeometry(35, 35);
var planeMaterial = new THREE.MeshPhongMaterial(
    {color: 0xffffff,
    map:floorTexture});
var plane = new THREE.Mesh(planeGeometry, planeMaterial);
plane.receiveShadow = true;
```

The only thing left to do is to define the number of times the texture is repeated for the X and Y axis with:

```
floorTexture.repeat.set(5,5);
wallTexture.repeat.set(3,2)
```

Note that the number of repetitions is independent of the size of the object, so that if we want to repeat it in equal size, we should calculate it based on the height and width of the object surface.

To create four walls, I've used the function ***clone*** and positioned them so that they form a square. Virtually all *Three.js* objects can be cloned.

```
scene.add(wall);
var wall1=wall.clone()
scene.add(wall1);
var wall2=wall.clone()
scene.add(wall2);
var wall3=wall.clone()
scene.add(wall3);

wall.position.z=-10;
wall1.position.z=10;
wall2.position.x=-9.5;
wall3.position.x=9.5;
wall2.rotation.y=0.5 * Math.PI;
wall3.rotation.y=0.5 * Math.PI;
```

To see the example code running or to download it, click here:

https://www.thefiveplanets.org/b01/c03/18-repeat-texture.html.

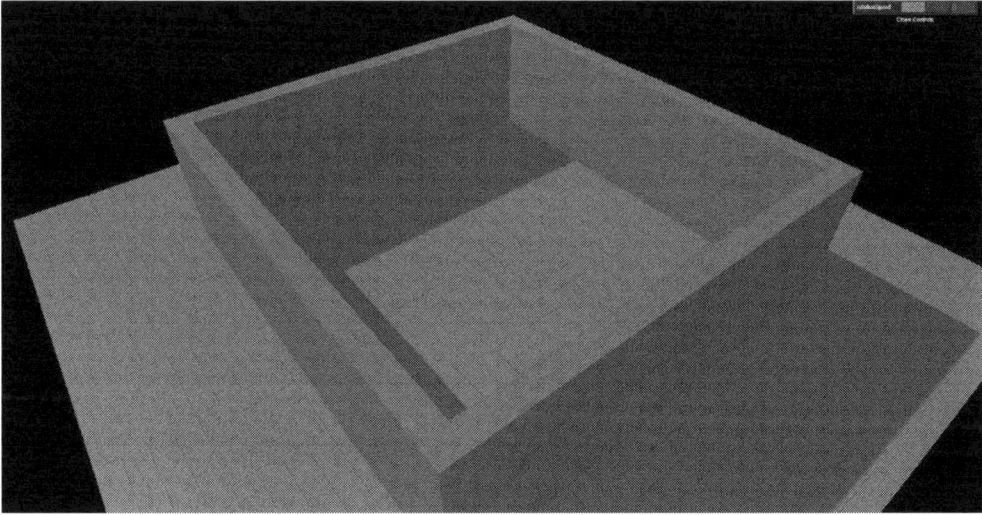

Fig. 3.33 Example of texture repetition.

Tip

For planes, cubes, or large geometric shapes that repeat textures, it's much more efficient to use *bufferGeometry* and its derived classes. You can find useful information about this in the next chapter.

TRANSPARENCIES

Using transparent materials is very simple. It merely requires modification of a couple of attributes of the materials: changing **transparent** to true and **opacity** to specify the degree of opacity of the material (*0* is completely transparent and *1* is completely opaque).

```
var wallMaterial = new THREE.MeshPhongMaterial(
    {color: 0xffffff,
    transparent:true,
    opacity:1});
```

We've used this effect repeatedly in some examples in the book.

But *Three.js* also lets you load transparent textures. This requires us to use images that support transparency, such as format *png*. To illustrate this, we've created a background with an image of a transparent shrub.

```
var grassTexture=textureLoader.load("../data/graphics/textures/vegetation/grass.png");
var grassGeometry = new THREE.PlaneGeometry(6, 6);
var grassMaterial = new THREE.MeshLambertMaterial(
    {color: 0xffffff,
```

```
        map:grassTexture,
        transparent:true,
        opacity:1,
        side: THREE.DoubleSide,
        depthWrite: false,
        depthTest: false });
var grass = new THREE.Mesh(grassGeometry, grassMaterial);
```

Notice that we've specified *side=THREE.DoubleSide* so that when the image rotates the plane is always visible. We've also specified *depthWrite=false* and *depthTest=false* so that by placing several transparent planes on top of each other, those behind are drawn. If this did not happen then the transparency effect would be diminished.

Fig. 3.34 Shrub with transparent background.

We've duplicated the plane 4 times, by placing them at the same point but rotating them so that there is a distance of 45 ° between the flat sections. This is how we create the impression of a shrub with volume.

```
var grass0=grass.clone();
scene.add(grass0);
var grass1=grass.clone();
scene.add(grass1)
grass1.rotation.y=0.25*Math.PI;
var grass2=grass.clone()
grass2.rotation.y=-0.25*Math.PI;
scene.add(grass2)
var grass3=grass.clone()
grass3.rotation.y=0.5*Math.PI;
scene.add(grass3)
```

To see the example code running or to download it you can click here:

https://www.thefiveplanets.org/b01/c03/19-transparent-texture.html

Fig. 3.35. Example of a transparent texture.

LIGHTS

Lights are instances of the class *THREE.light*, which in turn comes from *THREE.Object3D*. Lights allow objects be visible, they darken or lighten the colour of the objects (depending on how much light they receive) and they cast shadows, which is something we shall talk more about later. Lights only affects **THREE.MeshLambertMaterial** and **THREE.MeshPhongMaterial**, so other objects with other materials will always be visible when we use them.

There are different types of light, such as ambient light, which affects all objects equally and does not generate shadows. Or points of light, which are like bulbs placed at one point and the objects are affected by the distance at which they are located; the greater the distance the dimmer the illumination, and the shadows vary depending on the position of the object relative to the point of light.

Only *WebGL* supports some features of lights, such as shadows. Other types of *renders* do not have this ability.

Three.js includes many customization possibilities, which range from the colour of the lights to their intensity. Let us look at the list of the different types.

Ambient (THREE.AmbientLight) and directional (THREE.DirectionalLight) lighting

In our first contact with illumination we'll look at two types of lights: ambient (**THREE.AmbientLight**) and directional (**THREE.DirectcionalLight**) lighting.

The *ambient light* illuminates all sides of the objects there are in the scene, wherever they are. Their position and orientation are of no consequence and they will always be illuminated. It's therefore common to use a low intensity, just to ensure that the areas that receive no light are not completely black.

Directional lighting is like sunlight. The light rays are parallel with respect to each other and will influence our scene according to the direction of the vector we specify. The scene will be illuminated no matter how far away from the light source it is, but will always be at the angle we specify. This will make some faces light up whereas others will remain in darkness.

Directional light does not take into account whether there are objects in front of it. it's as if the light pierces through the figures and illuminates them from behind. Later we'll discuss shadows, as the projection of the shadow obscures the other figure.

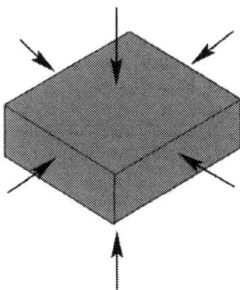

Fig. 3.36. Ambient lighting.

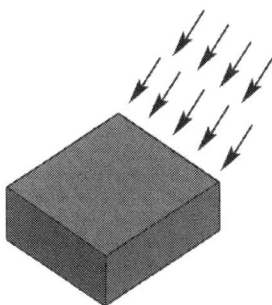

Fig. 3.37. Directional lighting.

Click this link to see an example of the two types of lights:
https://www.thefiveplanets.org/b01/c03/20-directional-ambient-light.html.

Let us see how the example works.

As a first step, we create light sources. For ambient light, we use **THREE.AmbientLight**, which only requires the colour of light in hexadecimal format and the illumination intensity. For example, a white light to simulate noon will have the following source (0xffffff).

```
var ambientLigth = new THREE.AmbientLight(0xffffff,0.4);
scene.add(lambientLight);
```

For sunlight, we use **THREE.DirectionalLight**, which accepts two parameters: colour and its intensity. It also accepts a third parameter, distance, but this affects the shadows, so we'll look at it afterwards. The direction of the light is defined by the vector created from **DirectionalLight.position** to **DirectionalLight.target.position**.

```
var directionalLight = new THREE.DirectionalLight(0xffffff,2);
directionalLight.position.set(10,20,20);
directionalLight.target.position.set(0,0,0);
```

```
scene.add(directionalLight);
```

Now we simply need to add figures and objects to see the lighting effect. In the first examples in the book we used the material *THREE.MeshBasicMaterial*, which ignores light, so that without adding lights we could see the objects. Now the figures we add are of other materials that alter their colour depending on the lighting: *THREE.MeshLambertMaterial* and *THREE.MeshPhongMaterial*. We've used the objects in the examples in this chapter for the composition.

Note that dynamically we change the colour and intensity of lights with the following code:

```
ambientLight.visible=control.ambientLight_visible;
ambientLight.color=new THREE.Color(control.ambientLight_color);
ambientLight.intensity=control.ambientLight_intensity;
directionalLight.visible=control.directionalLight_visible;
directionalLight.color=new THREE.Color(control.directionalLight_color);
directionalLight.intensity=control.directionalLight_intensity;
directionalLight.castShadow=control.directionalLight_castShadow;
if (control.directionalLight_move) {
    directionalLight.position.y = directionalLight.position.y
    * Math.cos(rotSpeed*0.5) + directionalLight.position.z
    * Math.sin(rotSpeed*0.5);
    directionalLight.position.z = directionalLight.position.z
    * Math.cos(rotSpeed*0.5) - directionalLight.position.y
    * Math.sin(rotSpeed*0.5);
}
```

In the following images, you can see the result of running the example by activating or deactivating the lights.

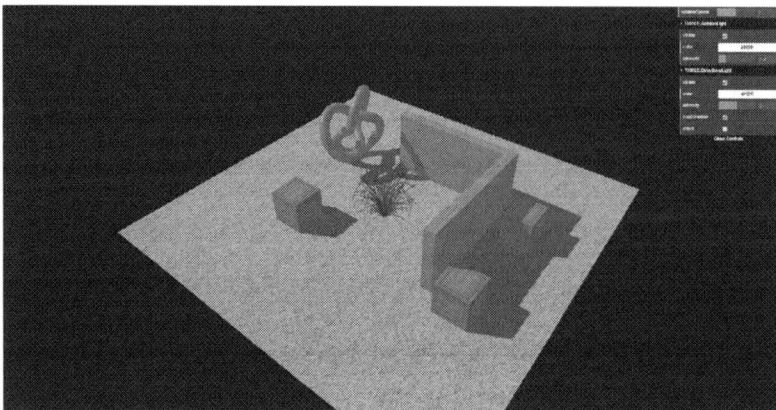

Fig. 3.38. With simultaneous ambient and directional light.

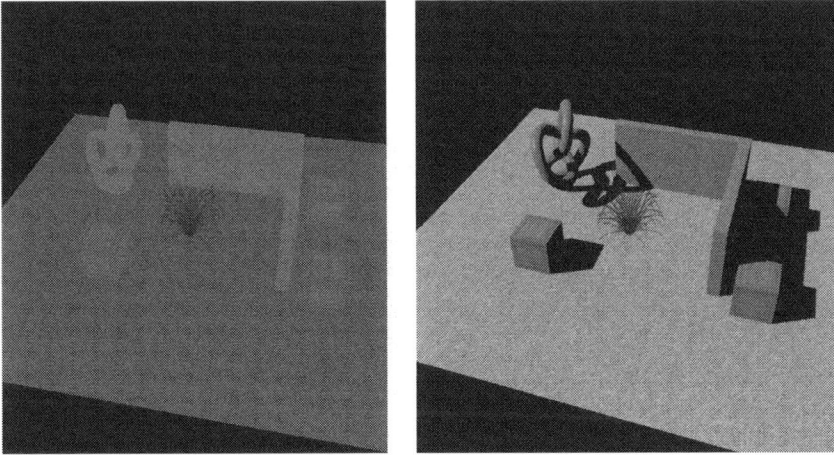

Fig. 3.39. Left: Only with ambient light activated. Right: Only with directional light activated.

Hemispheric light (THREE.HemisphereLight)

If we look at the sunlight outside, we see that the light does not really come from one direction. Part of the sunlight is reflected from the earth, which in turn bounces back into the atmosphere, while another part is scattered by the atmosphere. The result is a very soft light coming from lots of directions. In *Three.js*, we can create something similar with **THREE.HemisphereLight**.

The function of this light is similar to ambient light, designed to illuminate all faces of objects. To cast shadows, it needs to be combined with another light e.g. directional light, since hemispheric light does not generate shadows.

To see the effect of this type of light we've modified the example in the previous section to replace the directional light with hemispheric light (https://www.thefiveplanets.org/b01/c03/21-directional-hemisphere-light.html). In the example, we've included an interface to activate the hemispheric and directional light to see the differences and to see how they combine with each other. You can see the result in the following screenshot.

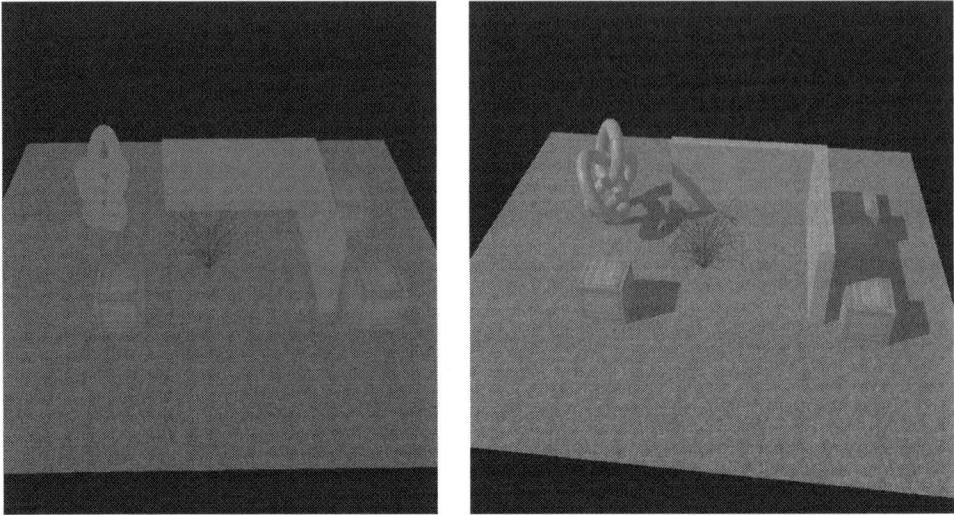

Fig. 3.40. Left: hemispheric light only. Right: directional and hemispherical light simultaneously.

The creation of **THREE.HemisphereLight** is similar to the creation of the other lights:

```
var hemisphereLight= new THREE.HemisphereLight ( 0xffffff, 0xffffff, 0.4);
hemisphereLight.position.set(0, 20, 0);
scene.add(hemisphereLigh);
```

The first parameter corresponds to the colour of the light of the sky, while the second establishes the colour of the light reflected from the ground. In both cases, we've set a white light. With the latter property, we control the light intensity. To achieve the best effect, it's better to place the light directly over the scene, in our case the position *(0, 20, 0)*.

In the example, we dynamically change the intensity and the colour of the light bounced off the ground and the sky with the following code:

```
hemisphereLight.visible=control.hemisphereLight_visible;
hemisphereLight.skyColor=new THREE.Color(control.hemisphereLight_skyColor);
hemisphereLight.groundColor=new THREE.Color(control.hemisphereLight_groundColor);
hemisphereLight.intensity=control.hemisphereLight_intensity;
```

You can use *THREE.HemisphereLight* as the main source of light, but it's more common to use this light source along with other types, for example *THREE.DirectionalLight,* since the latter can cast shadows. Note that in this case *THREE.HemisphereLight* will act like the ambient light as we saw in the previous section, but with a more spectacular effect.

In reality *THREE.HemisphereLight* acts like two *THREE.DirectionalLight objects*, one placed in the specified position and the other in exactly the opposite position.

Therefore, when *THREE.HemisphereLight* is used in a scene the object is illuminated from the top and from the opposite direction to create a more natural effect.

We can of course, also use two *THREE.DirectionalLight object*s instead. With appropriate parameterization, we can achieve the same effect as we can obtain with *THREE.HemisphereLight*. The added advantage is that multiple shadows are generated, one strong one and another weaker one in the opposite direction.

Point Light (THREE.PointLight) and Spot Light (THREE.SpotLight)

These types of lights are designed like light coming from a point in space and act as if they were light bulbs or spotlights. Both lights support the casting of shadows.

THREE.PointLight (colour, intensity = 1, distance = 8, decay = 1)

THREE.PointLight emanates from a specific point in space, like a light bulb. The light is projected in all directions and illuminates everything that is around it.

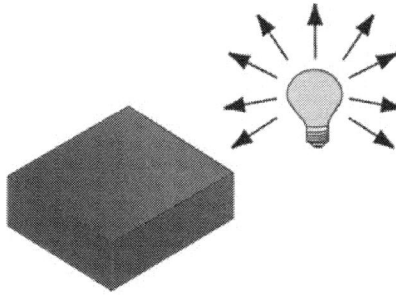

Fig. 3.41. PointLight lighting.

The parameters that we indicate when instantiating the class are the light colour, the intensity, the distance and the fading. The distance corresponds to the radius of the sphere, so that what is outside it will not be lit up. The fading is the amount of light that is attenuated over distance, and by default is 1.

To see how it behaves we've removed the lights in the example in the previous section, and instead have created a point of light (*THREE.PointLight*):

```
pointLight = new THREE.PointLight(0xffffff, 9, 20);
pointLight.position.set( 0, 5, 0 );
pointLight.castShadow = true;
scene.add(pointLight);
```

In addition, we've incorporated extremely soft ambient light, so that we can view objects that are hidden in the shadows, or outside the radius of the point light.

```
ambientLight = new THREE.AmbientLight(0xffffff,0.02);
scene.add(ambientLight);
```

To control the colour values, intensity, distance and dynamic dimming we've created an interface with *GUI.dat* and have introduced the following code in an animation loop:

```
pointLight.visible=control.pointLight_visible;
pointLight.color=new THREE.Color(control.pointLight_color);
pointLight.intensity=control.pointLight_intensity;
pointLight.distance=control.pointLight_distance;
pointLight.decay=control.pointLight_decay;
pointLight.castShadow=control.pointLight_castShadow;
```

The result of the example, along with the complete code, can be seen here: https://www.thefiveplanets.org/b01/c03/22-point-spot-light.html.

Fig. 3.42. Example with a point of light and a very weak ambient light.

THREE.SpotLight (colour, intensity = 1, distance = 8, angle = Math.PI / 3, penumbra = 1, decay = 1)

THREE.SpotLight emanates from a point in space in a specific direction. The light is projected in a cone shape, acting as if it were a spotlight. All objects outside the cone remain in the shadows.

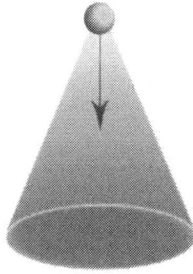

Fig. 3.43. Spot lighting (THREE.SpotLight).

The parameters for the spot light constructor are: colour, intensity, distance, angle, penumbra and decay. The distance corresponds to the height of the cone, that is to say, the distance between the tip of the cone and the centre of the circle of the base. The angle is formed between the line drawn from the tip of the cone to its base with the walls of the cone and its value is between 0 and 1.57 (i.e. an angle of 0 to 90 expressed in radians). The penumbra basically affects how light fades away as it moves away from the centre of the cone and approaches the walls. In the case of zero value, the circle drawn on the ground by projecting the light will look sharp and uniform, while in the case of value 1 it will fade gradually to darken completely. Fading is the amount of light that is attenuated over distance, and by default it has a value of 1.

For this light, unlike the previous one, we specify the direction toward which the spotlight points. In this case, we do not do it by rotating the light, but by indicating the property *target*.

You can see a complete example here: https://www.thefiveplanets.org/b01/c03/23-spot-light.html. Thus, the code we used to create the light is as follows.

```
spotLight = new THREE.SpotLight(0xffffff, 10, 100, 0.6, 0.5, 0);
spotLight.position.set (0, 15 , 0);
spotLight.target.position.set(0, 0 , 0);
spotLight.castShadow = true;
scene.add(spotLight);

lightHelper = new THREE.SpotLightHelper( spotLight );
scene.add(lightHelper);
```

Note that we've added a *helper (THREE.SpotLightHelper)* to see the cone that projects the light, which will make it easier to understand how it affects each parameter.

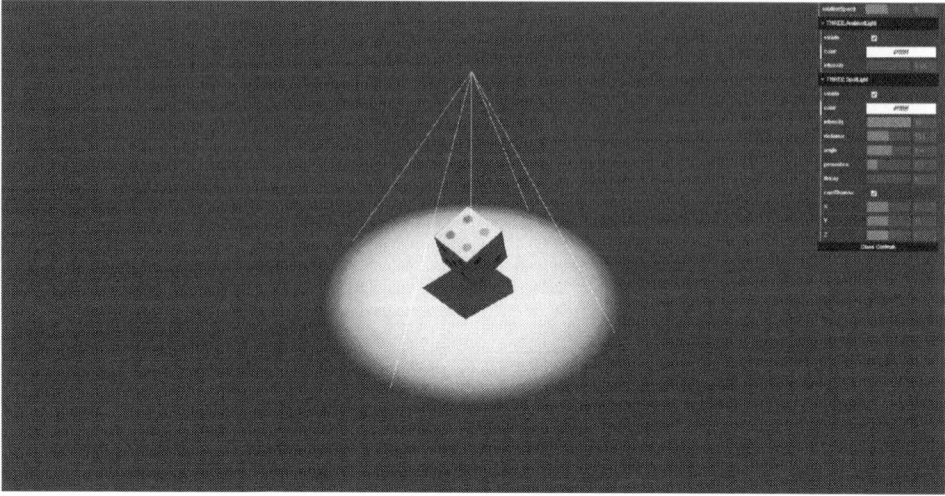

Fig. 3.44. Example of spotlight (THREE.SpotLight)

We use the following code to dynamically change the values of the intensity, colour, distance, angle, penumbra and position.

```
spotLight.visible=control.spotLight_visible;
spotLight.color = new THREE.Color(control.spotLight_color);
spotLight.intensity = control.spotLight_intensity;
spotLight.distance = control.spotLight_distance;
spotLight.angle = control.spotLight_angle;
spotLight.penumbra = control.spotLight_penumbra;
spotLight.decay = control.spotLight_decay;
spotLight.castShadow = control.spotLight_castShadow;
spotLight.position.set(control.spotLight_positionX,control.spotLight_positionY,control.spotLight_positionZ);
```

SHADOWS

Only some lights can cast shadows. *THREE.AmbientLight* and *THREE.HemisfereLight* are support lights that do not generate shadows, while *THREE.DirectionalLight*, *THREE.PointLight* and *THREE.SpotLight* project them, provided this functionality is explicitly activated. For this we must specify the property *shadowMap.enabled* in the *render* and the property *castShadow* in the lights, as shown in the following instructions:

```
renderer = new THREE.WebGLRenderer()
renderer.shadowMap.enabled=true;
...
directionalLight = new THREE.DirectionalLight(0xffffff, 2 );
directionalLight.castShadow = true;
...
pointLight = new THREE.PointLight(0xffffff, 9, 20 );
pointLight.castShadow = true;
```

```
...
spotLight = new THREE.SpotLight(0xffffff, 9, 15, Math.PI/3, 1, 1);
spotLight.castShadow = true;
```

But these instructions are not enough. By default, objects do not cast shadows, nor are affected by others, so we must activate these two properties for each figure in the scene.

castShadow > (*true* - the object casts a shadow on other objects, *false* - no shadow is shown).

receiveShadow > (*true* - the shadows are displayed on the surface of the object, *false* - the shadows are not projected onto the surface of the object and the object is illuminated).

For example:

```
var plane = new THREE.Mesh(planeGeometry, planeMaterial);
plane.receiveShadow = true;
var cube = new THREE.Mesh(cubeGeometry, cubeMaterial);
cube.castShadow = true;
cube.receiveShadow = true;
var wall = new THREE.Mesh(wallGeometry, wallMaterial);
wall.castShadow = true;
wall.receiveShadow = true;
```

You should remember that the shadows effects only the materials *THREE.MeshLambertMaterial* and *THREE.MeshPhongMaterial*.

You can see a complete example and run the code here: https://www.thefiveplanets.org/b01/c03/24-shadows.html. In the example, we've added several objects, materials and different types of light, which can be enabled or disabled dynamically.

Calculating real-time shadows can be very costly, depending mainly on the quality we want to display. It's therefore advisable to use techniques that restrict their use. For example, if we want to work with shadows in games, it's very common to activate *receiveShadow* just for the ground, while *castShadow* is activated for monsters and characters and some of the objects. This is how we reduce the amount of calculations.

Another possible improvement is to limit the area in which the shadows are displayed, so that only the objects next to the camera cast them.

With the following code, we create an imaginary cube that is projected in the direction of the light (from its position towards the target). Shadows will not be displayed outside the cube.

```
directionalLight = new THREE.DirectionalLight(0xffffff, 2 );
directionalLight.castShadow = true;
directionalLight.position.set(10, 20 , 20);
directionalLight.target.position.set(0, 0 , 0);
directionalLight.shadow.camera.near = 0;
directionalLight.shadow.camera.far = 50;
directionalLight.shadow.mapSize.width = 3 * 512;
directionalLight.shadow.mapSize.height = 3 * 512;
directionalLight.shadow.camera.top = 25;
directionalLight.shadow.camera.right = 25;
directionalLight.shadow.camera.left = -25;
directionalLight.shadow.camera.bottom = -25;
directionalLight.shadow.camera.visible = true;
scene.add(directionalLight);

directionalHelper = new THREE.CameraHelper( directionalLight.shadow.camera );
scene.add(directionalHelper);
```

In the code, we've included a helper (*THREE.CameraHelper*) that allows us to graphically define the area where the directional light generates shadows. The following image is the result of running the example, in which we can see the cube.

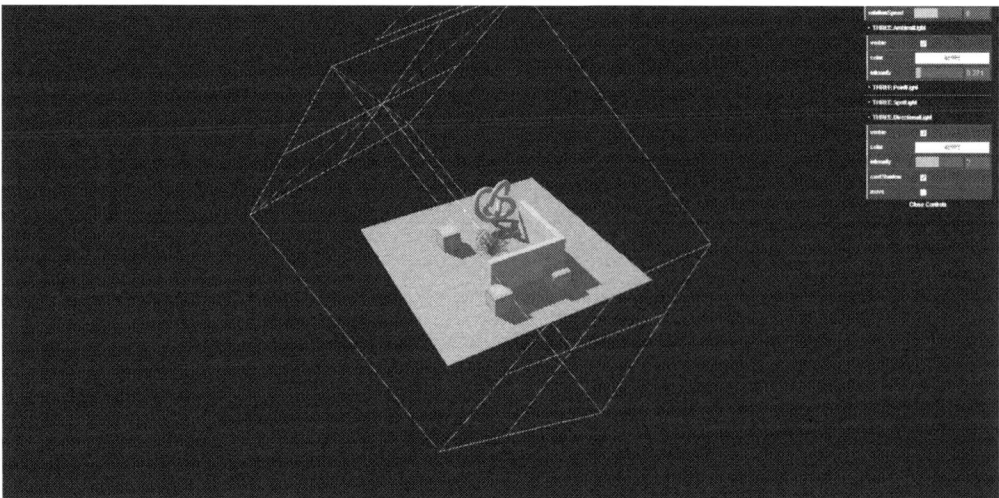

Fig. 3.45. Shadow Projection Cube for directional light.

To indicate the properties of the cube where the shadows are projected, we need access the value of the property *shadow.camera*, where the properties (*top, right, left,* and *bottom*) delimit the size of the upper and lower planes. *Near* and *far* specify the distance that the upper and lower planes are located with respect to the position of the light.

Tip

Note that, if we move the directional light with the camera, the shadows will only be displayed around the camera in a first-person game. This technique is discussed below.

C4 - THREEJS: CREATING OUR WORLD

At this point I think we are ready to start developing our game. In this chapter, we'll work on creating the map of the first location and animating some monsters.

LOAD EXTERNAL MODELS (LOADERS)

In this section, we'll learn the basics of how to load complex objects generated by *3D* editors. In later books, we'll explore these points in more detail and learn how to use some of them.

The basic geometric shapes that we've experimented with, work well for testing or to function as support for collision systems, for example, as we'll discuss later. But any serious game is likely to make heavy use of *3D* models created with specialized editors like *Blender, Maya, 3ds Max,* etc. These models should be loaded with the libraries provided by *Three.js* or should be exported to a native *Three.js* format through specific *plugins* to each editor.

There are many loaders for models in non-native formats, including *CM, OBJ, MTL, PLY, STL, UTF8, VRML and VTK*. These are found in the folder *"samples/js/loaders"*. Some of the formats support animations that can also be used in our scene.

When you load these models, they must often be resized and rotated, since there is no standard placement of the axes, nor of the measurements. Therefore, the position or scale that they are in depends on the program that was used to create them, or on the author. For example, *Blender* uses the Z axis for height and some creators use the object's centre as the home position, while the home position corresponds to the ground for others.

Similarly, we find models designed for use in traditional games, with heavy textures and with lots of animations. Therefore, to use them we must edit the textures to reduce their size and eliminate some animations. Likewise, if we use models by various authors, it's quite possible that the colours of the textures will not fit and we must edit them using a graphical editor like *Photoshop*.

The other element that we must deal with are the incompatibilities. For example, *Three.js* does not allow us to load *Collada* elements, which have a composite texture and are animated at the same time, since they display the object but not the animation.

Here is how to address some of the simplest challenges. In other books in the series we'll explore more advanced solutions.

Tip

Remember that libraries to load 3D models will not work on local files, so we must set up a server or configure the browser so that we can run the scenes locally. In *Chapter Two* we addressed a number of proposals to deal with the problem.

In the following sections, we'll focus on three types of loaders:

1.) The format *OBJ* and *MTL*. They use plain text files, which when we edit them can clearly distinguish the list of vertices and faces, and instructions to indicate the mapping of textures.
2.) The *collada* (*.dae*), which is a more elaborate format, also supports animations. Like the previous one, we can also open it with a text editor, since it's an *XML* file.
3.) And finally, we'll introduce *Three.js* own format, which describes the models using *JSON*. To generate these files from 3D editors we need to install a *plugin* designed specifically for the editor. *Three.js* includes extensions for *3ds Max*, *Maya* and *Blender* which allow us to export models in the format *JSON Three.js*. Unfortunately, these extensions have some limitations and are not compatible with some elements that they do not have on export.

These libraries do not have a standardized format, so they work slightly differently. Therefore, before we use one of the libraries, we must check the samples *demo* folder to see how they use it.

Format .OBJ (THREE.OBJLoader and THREE.MTLLoader)

A widely-supported standard is the OBJ format. With this format, the model is described with two different files. A file with the *.obj* extension which defines the geometry and a file with the *.mtl* extension which defines the material, and of course the texture files (* *.png, Jpg*). The load is asynchronous, so when calling the function to read it we must also provide a function that runs when it has finished loading and optionally a function to spot errors and another to manage the progress of the load.

Click the following link to see an example of it and download the code:
https://www.thefiveplanets.org/b01/c04/01-loadOBJ.html

Fig. 4.1. Example of an object .OBJ.

In the example code, we see that at the top of the page we've introduced two references to the JavaScript libraries. By default, the loaders are not part of the core of *Three.js* so they must be imported.

```
<script src="../frameworks/loaders/MTLLoader.js"></script>
<script src="../frameworks/loaders/OBJLoader.js"></script>
```

Secondly, we've created a specific function, ***loadOBJ***, to which we pass the following parameters: the path where the model is found, the name of the two files (the material and geometry), the scene where we want to add the object and the function to be executed once the object has been loaded successfully. Note that we do not call the function that creates the animation loop until the object is fully loaded, because, as we've already said, the function is asynchronous.

```
loadOBJ ("../data/models/castle/",
    "towerl.mtl",
    "towerl.obj",
    scene,
    function (object){
        tower=object;
        render();
});
```

If we examine the function code of ***loadOBJ*** we can see how we made two asynchronous calls to load the object and the material. In addition, we've created a function to monitor progress and another to monitor if an error occurs. In both cases, we write the result in the console. We could improve the progress function in a way that we inform the user how loading is progressing or by modifying the error handling function by providing a message in case of failure.

```
function loadOBJ (path, fileMaterial, fileOBJ, scene, fSuc, fFail) {
  var onProgress = function (xhr) {
    if (xhr.lengthComputable) {
      var percentComplete = xhr.loaded / xhr.total * 100;
      console.log(Math.round(percentComplete, 2) + '% downloaded');
    }
  };
  var onError = function (xhr) {
    if (fFail) {fFail(xhr);}
    console.log('ERROR');
  };
  var mtlLoader = new THREE.MTLLoader();
  mtlLoader.setPath(path);
  mtlLoader.load(fileMaterial, function (materials) {
    materials.preload();
    var objLoader = new THREE.OBJLoader();
    objLoader.setMaterials(materials);
    objLoader.setPath(path);
    objLoader.load(fileOBJ, function (object) {
      scene.add(object);

      ...
      fSuc(object);
    }, onProgress, onError);
  });
};
```

Enabling shadows and changing object properties

In the returned object shadow casting is turned off. If we try to activate it with the instruction *object.castShadow = true* we see that it has no effect, which is because the loader by default returns an object of the *THREE.Group* class and not *THREE.Mesh.*

THREE.Group is a group of objects. In other words, it may contain objects of various types, *THREE.Mesh, THREE.Camera, THREE.Audio,* etc. In reality, it may include any object that inherits from *THREE.Object3D.*

Not only that, but *THREE.Group* also inherits from *THREE.Object3D,* so you can position it within the scene, rotate it on its axis, scale, etc. If we remember, we said that we can add another object in any object of *THREE.Object3D* class, so that a structure is created in tree form. To traverse all the descendants of an object (regardless of level) use the function ***traverse,*** as shown in the following code:

```
object.traverse(function (child) {
```

```
    if (child instanceof THREE.Mesh) {
        ...
    }
});
```

In addition, we can see what class it's from by using ***instanceof***. In this case, we are interested in *THREE.Mesh*. Thus, we are ready to activate the casting of shadows. Notice that we've not included ***recieveShadow*** because in this case, we'll not activate the reception of shadows for objects in order to reduce the complexity of the calculations. So, the final code is as follows:

```
object.traverse(function (child) {
    if (child instanceof THREE.Mesh) {
        child.castShadow = true;
    }
});
object.position.set(0, 0, 0);
```

In the *rendering* loop, we've applied the same principle to modify the transparency:

```
tower.traverse(function (child) {
    if (child instanceof THREE.Mesh) {
        child.material.transparent = true;
        child.material.opacity = control.opacity;
    }
});
```

This same technique can be used to correct or change other elements. In the following example, we've loaded a model of a house, which is designed only to be seen from the outside and thus by placing the camera inside the house this makes the walls and ceiling invisible. By using the previous technique, we may specify that the material of the object is double-sided and so have a house with the interiors. You can see an example here: https://www.thefiveplanets.org/b01/c04/02-loadOBJ-house.html

```
tower.traverse(function (child) {
        if (child instanceof THREE.Mesh) {
            child.material.transparent = true;
            child.material.opacity = control.opacity;
            child.material.side= + THREE.DoubleSide;
        }
});
```

Solving problems

There are many problems that can occur when loading the object and which make it invisible or displayed without texture.

Scale

If an object has been loaded successfully, but is not visible in the scene, it may be due to size. If it's too large it will wrap the scene and it will not be visible, whereas if it's too small it will appear hidden. It seems like an obvious problem to solve, but there are plenty of messages in the forums asking for help to fix it.

Here we can see an example of a change in scale, by halving its size:

```
object.scale.x = object.scale.y = object.scale.z = 0.5;
```

Troubleshoot problems with the web server

As we've stated, if the code is run locally, the objects will not be loaded without first applying the solutions already outlined in Chapter Two. Even if we use a Web server we may still not be able to visualize the scene and this may be a permission and configuration problem. So, for the server to be able to deliver files with extension (*.obj* or *.mtl*) we must specify the encoding and the mime.

For example, to configure a WEB server of the *.NET* type we must modify the file "*web.config*" with the following instructions:

```
<system.webServer>
  <staticContent>
    <mimeMap fileExtension=".obj" mimeType="application/octet-stream" />
    <mimeMap fileExtension=".mtl" mimeType="application/octet-stream" />
    ...
  </staticContent>
</system.webServer>
```

The object is not displaying the texture.

When you load the object, the texture is often not displayed. As we've stated, this format is defined using different files, one for geometry, one for materials and others for images of textures separately. In the file that describes the materials (*.mtl*) there are references to the names of texture files.

If we open the file *.mtl* with a text editor, the names of the texture files may be specified with an absolute path "*c:\\MyModels\Tower*" and therefore the loader will not be able to interpret it. In these cases, it's best to move the texture to the same folder as the object and specify a relative path to the texture in the file *.mtl*.

```
newmtl tower1_material
illum 2
Ka 0.588000 0.588000 0.588000
Kd 0.588000 0.588000 0.588000
Ks 0.000000 0.000000 0.000000
Ns 10.000000
map_Kd tower1.jpg
```

Another possible problem is that the file *.obj* also contains a reference to the file path that defines the materials *.mtl*. This can also be in absolute format and even contain errors. The procedure to solve it's the same as for file *.mtl*, as it can also be opened with a text editor.

Below you can see a part of the file *tower1.obj* as an example. Note that the line "*mtllib tower1.mtl*" serves to specify the file that defines the materials. While the line "*usemtl tower1_material*" specifies the defined material used, which matches the name on the file *tower1.mtl* in "***newmtl tower1_material***".

Another problem we've found is that the material name does not match in both files. For instance, Visual Studio has a *3D* editor but when we save the object in OBJ format it destroys the reference. This bug is from the 2012 version and still exists in the 2016 version, but we can fix it easily by editing text files.

```
mtllib tower1.mtl
usemtl tower1_material

v 3.892117 0.605004 4.398189
v 3.169382 8.733324 3.607677

..

vn 0.000000 0.096800 0.995304
vn 0.000000 0.067402 0.997726

..

vt 0.706900 0.034800
vt 0.685800 0.267600

..

f 1/1/1 2/2/2 3/3/2
f 4/4/3 5/5/4 6/6/4
```

You can learn more about the OBJ format here:
https://en.wikipedia.org/wiki/Wavefront_.obj_file.

Slow loading time or a reduction of frames during running.

Loading the object can be time-consuming, which may be because the images for textures are heavy and are not suitable for use on the web. To solve the problem, we'll use a graphical editor like *Photoshop* and will reduce the size of the image.

It's also convenient to use a compressed format such as *jpg*. If we change the extension of the images, we'll modify the file *.mtl* to point to the correct textures.

Textures, range, colours.

When we incorporate objects made by different artists in the same scene, it's likely that colours textures, or their range of colours will not match. To fix this it's not necessary to use a 3D object editor. It can be done with a graphic editor like *Photoshop* to edit the colours and even add some details.

Collada fromat .DAE (THREE.ColladaLoader) and object animations

Collada (**COLLA***borative* **D***esign* **A***ctivity*) is an open format defined by *XML* and is designed to represent scenes in *3D*. Collada documents describing the models are *XML* files, usually identified with a *.dae* (*digital asset exchange*) file extension.

Unlike the format *.OBJ,* it supports not only 3D objects, but also supports full scenes with animated objects, lights, cameras and even allows defining the physical properties of the object for managing physics and collisions.

We've created a small example in which we load one of the monsters that we'll use in the game to illustrate how *collada* objects load. This example features a kind of alien dog that has just one type of animation to simulate walking. You can see the example in operation here: https://www.thefiveplanets.org/b01/c04/03-loadDAE.html

There are basically, two types of object animation. The first is animation by transformation (*morph*), by which the vertices of the object move, transforming the object into a different one. In this case, we provide a collection of vertices equal to the number of vertices of the original object, so that each vertex moves from its original position to its new position. This type of animation is optimal for facial expressions. The second method is animation by skeleton, in which a series of bones, which are linked to groups of vertices of the object and the joints between bones, are defined. This animation is created by moving the bones, so that animations are created by providing the position and orientation of the bones over time.

In this book, we'll not discuss animations. Instead we'll explore this topic in the second book of the collection. We'll just learn to activate them. In the example, the monster has been animated by a skeleton with 21 bones, as shown in the accompanying images.

Fig. 4.2. Example of loading .DAE object.

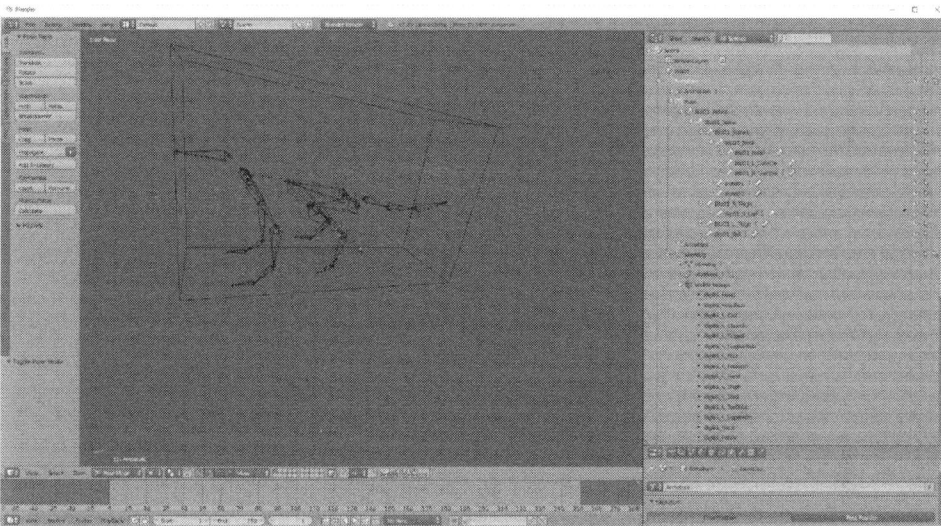

Fig. 4.3. Example of the skeleton used to animate the .DAE object.

Let us look at how the example works. As in the previous case, we must incorporate JavaScript libraries for reading the objects, but in this case we must do this with the *collada* format. As it's an animated object with a skeleton we added three additional libraries for managing animation:

```
<script src="../frameworks/loaders/ColladaLoader.js"></script>
<script src="../frameworks/loaders/collada/Animation.js"></script>
<script src="../frameworks/loaders/collada/AnimationHandler.js"></script>
<script src="../frameworks/loaders/collada/KeyFrameAnimation.js"></script>
```

To load the object, we've created a ***loadDAE*** function in which the parameters specified are: the relative path where our model is located, the **.dae* file name, the scene in which to add the object and finally the function to be called when the object is loaded. As in the rest of the loaders, the process is asynchronous so the function of starting the animation loop "*render*" is not invoked until loading is completed.

```
loadDAE ("../data/models/monsters/",
    "aliendog.dae",
    scene, function (obj){
        monster=obj;
        render();
});
```

As we've stated, the **.dae* file allows us to store complete scenes, cameras, lights, etc. The returned object includes the property **scene**, which allows access to an object of *THREE.Group.* type. From here on, the use of the object is very similar to that which we've seen in the previous section, where we analysed the *.OBJ* format. We can directly alter the position, orientation, scale or descendants when searching for *THREE.Mesh* instances to change certain properties such as the shadows.

```
function loadDAE (path, fileOBJ, scene, fSuc, fFail) {
    var loader = new THREE.ColladaLoader();
    var onProgress = function (xhr) {    };
    var onError = function (xhr) { if (fFail) { fFail(xhr); } };
    loader.load(path+fileOBJ, function (collada) {
        var object = collada.scene;
        // Correct scale
        object.scale.x = object.scale.y = object.scale.z = 0.005;
        // Correct head orientation
        object.rotateY(-Math.PI / 2);
        // Correct horizontal orientation
        object.rotateX(-Math.PI / 2);
        object.updateMatrix();
        object.position.set(0, 0, 0);

        // Enable shadows
        object.traverse(function (child) {
            if (child instanceof THREE.Mesh) {
                child.castShadow = true;
              }
            if (child instanceof THREE.SkinnedMesh) {
                var animation = new THREE.Animation(child, child.geometry.animation);
                animation.play();
            }
        });
        object.castShadow = true;
        scene.add(object);
```

```
    fSuc(object);
  }, onProgress, onError);
};
```

Activation of object animation

As we've stated, the model contains animation to simulate the movement of walking. By default, the animation is not automatically activated. We must do this manually.

The first step is to find all objects susceptible to animation, which we do with the function *travers,* and which runs through all descendants. In this case, we are only concerned with *THREE.SkinnedMesh* type of objects, which in turn inherit from *THREE.Mesh* but include the logic to animate them through a skeleton.

To achieve this, we've introduced the following lines just after the object has been loaded.

```
object.traverse(function (child) {
    if (child instanceof THREE.SkinnedMesh) {
        var animation = new THREE.Animation(child, child.geometry.animation);
        animation.play();
    }
    ....
}
```

Anyway, apart from creating animation and including it to the global list of animations to process with *animation.play()*, there is still one step left. In the recursive function of *rendering* the scene must include *THREE.AnimationHandler.update(delta)*. This instruction is responsible for updating all animation that has been activated. The parameter *delta* contains the time that has passed since you last ran the function. This time is that allows the animation not to run too fast or too slow.

```
function render() {
    var delta = clock.getDelta();
    ....
    THREE.AnimationHandler.update(delta);
    requestAnimationFrame(render);
    renderer.render(scene, camera);
}
```

Enabling shadows and changing object properties

Activating shadows or modifying the properties of the object is very similar to what we've seen in the *.OBJ* format. Therefore, if we try to activate it with the instruction *object.castShadow = true* we'll see that this has no effect. To do successfully activate them we must use the same technique that we used for animation, by running through all the descendants of the object and looking for those that are instances of *THREE.Mesh* class and activating the property *castShadow*. Optionally we can activate *receiveShadow* if we want the object to also be affected by shadows:

```
object.traverse(function (child) {
    if (child instanceof THREE.Mesh) {
        child.castShadow = true;
    }
});
object.position.set(0, 0, 0);
```

We used the same procedure to modify transparency.

```
monster.traverse(function (child) {
    if (child instanceof THREE.Mesh) {
        child.material.transparent = true;
        child.material.opacity = control.opacity;
    }
});
```

Solving problems

As was the case with load objects in .OBJ format, there are many problems that may arise, which affect visibility and functionality: the textures of the objects, loading times, etc. Many of the solutions are like those we've already seen, as the *collada* format can be edited with a text editor.

Scale

In the example that we've used, the loaded monster is much greater in size than the tower or the house we loaded in the example above, and when added it appears lying down. We used the following code to adjust the size and rotate the object to place it in a natural position:

```
var object = collada.scene;
//Correct scale
object.scale.x = object.scale.y = object.scale.z = 0.005;
//Correct head orientation
object.rotateY(-Math.PI / 2);
//Correct horizontal orientation
object.rotateX(-Math.PI / 2);
object.updateMatrix();
```

Troubleshoot problems with the web server

As with the format *.OBJ*, if we execute the code locally, the object will not be charged without first applying the solutions already outlined in Chapter Two. However, if we use a WEB server it's possible that it may continue not to be displayed due to problems with permissions and configuration. We must specify the encoding and the mime so that the server may deliver files with extensions (*.dae*).

For example, to configure a *WEB* server of a *.NET* type we must modify the file "*Web.config*" with the following instructions:

```
<system.webServer>
 <staticContent>
  <mimeMap fileExtension=".dae" mimeType="application/octet-stream" />

      ...
 </staticContent>
</system.webServer>
```

The object is not displaying the texture.

Another problem occurs when we load the object and the texture is not displayed. The problem may be because the file defining the object (*.dae*) contains the reference to the texture files names.

If we open the *.dae* file with a text editor, the names of the texture files may be specified with an absolute path "*c:\\ MyMmodels\Monster*", and therefore the loader will not be able to interpret them. It's best to move the texture to the same folder as the object and specify a relative path to the images of the textures. For example, we can locate the following piece of code where the textures are specified by opening the file *aliendog.dae*:

```
<library_images>
   <image id="aliendog.jpg" name="aliendog_jpg">
    <init_from>./aliendog.jpg</init_from>
   </image>
</library_images>
```

Slow loading time or a reduction of frames during running.

One of the problems that may arise when loading the object is that it takes a very long time and the animation goes very slowly even after it loads. This may be due to a variety of causes. For example, there may be too many or too detailed animations. On the internet, we can download many characters with animations, which run, fight, walk, cast spells, dance etc. The resulting object ends up using a lot of megabytes. Any object that has more than one pair, such as one with 60 megabytes, will be very heavy as a result. In this case, if there are many animations, we must select only those that we'll use, and discard the rest. And for those that we select, we must reduce the number of transitions.

We'll use a program for 3D editing that supports *collada* animated objects. Explaining how to do this goes beyond the objectives of this book, so we'll deal with it in another book in the collection.

Another cause of slowness, may be because the images for the textures are very heavy and are not suitable for use on the web. We've already seen the solution to this problem: downsizing with a graphical editor like *Photoshop,* but also using a compressed format such as *jpg.* If we change the extension of the images with a text editor we'll modify the *.dae* file so that it points to the correct textures.

Native format of three.js

Finally, the last way to load customised objects we'll discuss is the native *Three.js* form. In this case the models are stored in *JSON* format, so they are easily modified with a text editor. The built-in loaders allow us to read objects not only by their geometry and materials, but also other objects such as lights, cameras, and even arbitrary resources. This format also allows the use of animated objects with both the transformation technique (*morph*) and skeleton.

To generate objects in this model we have a very basic editor on the same page *threejs.org*, which can be accessed here: http://threejs.org/editor/.

Fig. 4.4. THREE.JS native editor.

From the editor, we can create objects from scratch or import others created in formats such as *DAE, OBJ, 3DS*, etc. After completing the changes, we can save in native *three.js* files (JSON) with the export menu options.

In addition, different *plugins* have been created which we can install in programs such as *3ds Max, Maya and Blender,* so that we can save the models and scenes directly in *Three.js* format (*JSON*) from our favourite editor rather than doing it in native format. Explaining the process in detail is beyond the scope of this book but the issue will be discussed subsequently in the collection.

In fact, we are not going to use the *JSON* format at all for the first version of the game. Instead we'll only use the *OBJ* format and when we need an animated object we'll use the *DAE* format.

To illustrate its use, we've exported the model of the house that we used earlier in *JSON* format. In this case, we've done it by using *blender,* after installing the *plugin.* You can see the result and download the code at https://www.thefiveplanets.org/b01/c04/04-loadJSON.html

Fig. 4.5. Example of loading three.js native object.

In this case, it's not necessary to include a library to use the loader, as it's already part of the core. Like *ColladaLoader* and *OBJLoader*; *JSONLoader* uses an asynchronous reading method. That is, we must specify the function that will be called once loading is completed, and we can optionally include two additional functions, one for error handling and another to show the progress of loading. The code has been encapsulated in a specific function, ***loadJSON,*** which we pass the URL of the object to be loaded, the scene where we are adding it and the function to call when finished.

```
function loadJSON (fileOBJ, scene, fSuc,fFail) {
    var onProgress = function (xhr) {
        if (xhr.lengthComputable) {
            var percentComplete = xhr.loaded / xhr.total * 100;
            console.log(Math.round(percentComplete, 2) + '% downloaded');
```

```
            }
    };
    var onError = function (xhr) {
            if (fFail) {fFail(xhr);}
            console.log('ERROR');
    };
    var loader = new THREE.JSONLoader();
            loader.load(fileOBJ, function(model, material) {
                    var mesh = new THREE.Mesh(model, material[0]);
                    mesh.castShadow = true;
                    mesh.receiveShadow = true;
                    scene.add(mesh);
                    fSuc(mesh);
        }, onProgress, onError);
};
```

Note that the function ***load*** is a little different from the two previous cases, since it receives the geometry of the object as the first parameter and returns a second parameter with an *array* of the materials. To call it we used the following code and we call our function of *rendering* of the scene once the model has loaded, as in the previous cases.

```
loadJSON ("../data/models/json/house.json", scene, function (obj){
    house=obj;
    house.scale.x=house.scale.z=1.5;
    house.updateMatrix();
    render();
});
```

FOG

Now that we know how to load objects, it's important to learn the concept of fog. When we create a scene, and add the camera we specify the viewing distance, that is, from at what distance the objects no longer appear in the camera. The more detailed our world, the more performance problems we have if we represent our scene for a far distance.

An unpleasant effect appears with objects appearing suddenly as we move when representing landscapes where we move around. They may even appear in pieces.

The classes *THREE.Fog* and *THREE.FogExp2* allow us to hide these problems, since it allows objects to fade to the colour we specify. If the colour is the same as the background then objects do not appear immediately, but will take on colour as we get closer. This effect allows us to simulate atmospheric fog, the effect of pollution in cities or sand suspended in the air in the desert, for example.

There are two types of fog that we can add to the scene:

Linear fog - THREE.Fog (colour, start, end)

Fog becomes denser in a linear manner, just like it does with the atmospheric phenomenon. The parameters specified are the colour of the fog, the distance at which objects begin to gain colour and the distance at which objects appear fully collared, so initially only the silhouette is visible with the colour of the fog. By establishing the same background colour as that of the fog we achieve the effect of fading.

```
scene.fog (new THREE.Fog (0xffffff, 0, 100);
renderer.setClearColor(scene.fog.color, 1);
```

You can see an example of linear fog here:
https://www.thefiveplanets.org/b01/c04/05-fog.html

Fig. 4.6. Example of linear fog.

Exponential fog - THREE.FoxExp2 (colour, density)

Fog becomes denser in an exponential manner. The parameters specified are the colour and the speed at which density increases (default 0.00025).

```
scene.fog (new THREE.FogExp2 (0xffffff, 0.00025);
renderer.setClearColor(scene.fog.color, 1);
```

You can see an example of exponential fog here:
https://www.thefiveplanets.org/b01/c04/06-fogexp2.html

Tip

We can specify which objects we want the fog to affect and which ones we do not want the fog to affect. To do this we must change the material property *fog* from true to false.

```
obj.material.fog = true;
```

CREATING THE BASE FOR THE GAME

At this point we have enough knowledge to create the base of game that will allow us to define the first location of the map. As specified at the beginning of the book the aim is to create a basic role-play game, in first person, so that from now on the examples will be focussed towards this goal. To facilitate the development of the game and the understanding of it we've divided the HTML code in multiple files, separating the HTML and JavaScript code. Therefore, we've created the following folder structure:

📁 *data*: In this folder, we've included graphics, textures, *3D* models, fonts, ambient music, sounds, etc. In other words, we've included all the data files to build the examples and the game.

   📁 *fonts*
   📁 *graphics*
      📁 *textures*
   📁 *models*
      ....

📁 *framework*: In this folder, you will find the *Three.js, JQuery, stats.js, dat.gui.js* libraries that we've introduced throughout the book. The aim is that they serve as a repertoire to the external libraries.

📁 *core*: Here are the JavaScript files that are part of the core of the examples and the game that we are writing. As we progress in the development of new examples and of the game we'll incorporate new subfolders and files. Initially we added the following files:

   📁 *world*: In this folder, we'll include the support files needed to create the initial scene, the map, the sky and elements of nature of our locations among other things. Initially we started with the following files:

      📄 *world_v01.js*: This is responsible for creating the basic elements of the scene and includes the animation loop and rendering of the scene.

      📄 *groud_v01.js*: This creates the basic ground for the game where we'll be able to move around.

   📁 *controls*: Basically, this includes controls to move the player with the keyboard, mouse or joystick. We initially included a controller that moves the camera along a predetermined path, which will allow us to simulate the player, seeing from a first-person perspective. In the next chapter, we'll explore the interaction with the mouse and keyboard.

- 🗎 **_controls_path_v01.js_**: This defines the class _$CONTROLS.PathControls_ which moves an object along a predetermined route.

In the names of the files you will see that we've added **_v01_** to specify the version. As we improve the code we'll change the name to **_v02_**, **_v03_** etc.

We can see a complete example of the new structure by creating a ground map, for which we've created a plane with a ground texture, which has foliage that will be periodically repeated.

You can see the complete example and download it here:
https://www.thefiveplanets.org/b01/c04/07-ground.html

If you open the main file (**_07-ground.html_**) you will see the following code:

```
<!DOCTYPE html>
<html xmlns="http://www.w3.org/1999/xhtml">
<head>
  <title>The Five Planets</title>
  <meta http-equiv="content-type" content="text/html;charset=utf-8" />
  <style>
        body {
                width:100%;
                height:100%;
                padding:0;
                margin:0;
                overflow:hidden;
        }
</style>
<link rel="stylesheet" type="text/css" href="../css/screen.css"/>

<!-- LOAD JQUERY & REQUIERE -->
<script src="../frameworks/require.min.js"></script>
<script src="../frameworks/jquery-2.0.3.min.js"></script>

<!-- LOAD THREE.JS -->
<script src="../frameworks/three.min.js" defer></script>
<script src="../frameworks/renders/projector.js" defer></script>
<script src="../frameworks/loaders/DDSLoader.js" defer></script>
<script src="../frameworks/loaders/MTLLoader.js" defer></script>
<script src="../frameworks/loaders/OBJLoader.js" defer></script>
<script src="../frameworks/loaders/ColladaLoader.js" defer></script>
<script src="../frameworks/loaders/collada/Animation.js" defer></script>
<script src="../frameworks/loaders/collada/AnimationHandler.js" defer></script>
```

```html
<script src="../frameworks/loaders/collada/KeyFrameAnimation.js" defer></script>

<!-- LOAD DAT.GUI & STATS-->
<script src="../frameworks/dat.gui.min.js" defer></script>
<script src="../frameworks/stats.js" defer></script>

<!-- GAME FILES-->
<script src="../core/controls/controls_path_v01.js" defer></script>
<script src="../core/world/world_v01.js" defer></script>
<script src="../core/world/ground_v01.js" defer></script>

<script>
$(document).ready(function () {
  $WORLD.init3D({}, function () {
          $WORLD.map = {
                  "x":256,
                  "z":256,
                  "ground": {
                          "type":"basic",
                          "texture":"../data/graphics/textures/terrain/grass1.jpg",
                          "resX":2,
                          "resY":2
                  }
          };
          $WORLD.drawGround();
          var path=new THREE.CatmullRomCurve3 ([
                  new THREE.Vector3(5, 2, 50),
                  new THREE.Vector3(9, 2, 40),
                  new THREE.Vector3(15, 2, 55),
                  new THREE.Vector3(50, 2, 5),
                  new THREE.Vector3(30, 2, 5),
                  new THREE.Vector3(35, 2, 50),
                  new THREE.Vector3(43, 2, 27),
                  new THREE.Vector3(50, 2, 33),
                  new THREE.Vector3(5, 2, 50)])
          $WORLD.controls = new $CONTROLS.PathControls ($WORLD.camera, path,
          {"velocity":2});
          $WORLD.controls.showPath();
          $WORLD.addToListUpdate ($WORLD.controls)
          $WORLD.showStats();
          $WORLD.startAnimation();
  });
})

</script>
</head>
```

```
<body>
</body>
</html>
```

If we analyse the file we see that we declare the external JavaScript libraries at the top (*three.min.js*, *require.min.js*, *jquery-2.0.3.min.js*, *dat.gui.min.js*, *stats.js*, ...). We've included the library *JQuery* amongst these, which makes handling events and DOM elements easier. In the example, we've only used it to trigger our code once all the JavaScript and CSS files have loaded: "*$(Document).ready (function () {...*". Later we'll use it to create the user interface.

In the code, we begin by calling *$WORLD.init3D*, which creates the *render* object and the scene. Note that one of the parameters is the function we'll execute when we've finished creating the object scene and the basic preparations. This is the technique we'll habitually use as it's a way to guarantee the execution order and it allows the code not to be run until the asynchronous calls are completed.

With *$WORLD.map* we specify the map size and its characteristics. For now, we only specify the size and graphic texture. The function *$WORLD.drawGround()* is responsible for adding the ground to the scene.

The instruction *$WORLD.controls = new $CONTROLS.PathControls ($WORLD.camera, path, {"velocity":2})* creates a control that is responsible for moving the camera along a predefined path and with *$WORLD.controls.showPath()* we make the path visible in order to facilitate understanding of the example. Note we've defined the path with *THREE.CatmullRomCurve3* that creates a curve, which passes through the array of points that we facilitate to the constructor.

With *$WORLD.addToListUpdate ($WORLD.controls)* we add the control to the list of items to be updated regularly. This feature will allow us to add the items we want to update over time like the monsters, fireballs, etc.

The instruction *$WORLD.showStats()* creates the statistics box at the top of the screen, and in this way, we can see how the design decisions that we take affect performance.

Finally, and most importantly, is the function that triggers the animation loop that will render the scene and refresh the camera movement: *$WORLD.startAnimation()*.

Improving the animation loop (world_v01.js)

If we open the file *world_v01.js* we see the casing of what will be the graphic engine of the game, which we'll improve and expand as we move through the chapters. In this file, we define the object *$WORLD* which provides the basis for creating the scene and controls the updates of all the elements over time (the famous rendering loop).

The properties and main functions are defined as follows:

Methods of $WORLD

$WORLD.init3D(oPars, fSucces, fFail): This function is responsible for creating the render, the basic camera, ambient light, preparing loaders and creating the scene.

$WORLD.showStats(): This creates a box at the top left to display statistics, such as frames per second and memory consumed so that we can optimize these parameters.

$WORLD.startAnimation(): This starts the animation and rendering loop.

$WORLD.pauseAnimation(): This pauses the animation and rendering loop.

$WORLD.animate(): This function is called regularly, ideally 60 times per second and is responsible for updating all screen elements. In other words, it moves the camera according to the player's position, updates the position of the monsters and characters on screen, updates animations, etc. This function will never be called directly. Instead, the navigator will execute it.

$WORLD.addToListUpdate(obj): This inserts an object into the list of objects that the function *animate* must update. The object must contain a method called *update* with a parameter: *delta* - the time passed since the last call. In ideal circumstances, the method will be called 60 times per second, the time parameter allows to adjust the animation for when the frequency is lower.

Properties of $WORLD

$WORLD.distance: This specifies the viewing distance that is the distance at which objects are no longer visible.

$WORLD.scene: This points to the *scene* object.

$WORLD.map: This contains the definition of the map in JSON format. It specifies how it is the sky, the ground where the buildings are located, walls, etc.

$WORLD.controls: This contains the object that is responsible for moving the camera and managing the movement of the player. In the next chapter of the book we'll see different controllers.

Here we see the code file ***world_v01.js*** which defines the object *$WORLD* (the first version):

```javascript
var $WORLD = $WORLD || {};
$WORLD.distance = 80;
$WORLD.renderer = null;
$WORLD.scene = null;
$WORLD.clock = null;
$WORLD.map=null;
$WORLD.controls=null;
$WORLD._objUpdate = [];

$WORLD.init3D = function(oPars, fSuc, fFail) {

    var renderer = new THREE.WebGLRenderer();
    renderer.shadowMap.enabled = true;
    renderer.shadowMap.type = THREE.PCFSoftShadowMap;
    renderer.setSize(window.innerWidth, window.innerHeight);
    document.body.appendChild(renderer.domElement);
    $WORLD.renderer = renderer;
    $WORLD.scene = new THREE.Scene();

    $WORLD.camera = new THREE.PerspectiveCamera(
    75, window.innerWidth / window.innerHeight, 0.1, $WORLD.distance);
    $WORLD.camera.position.set(0, 2, 0);
    $WORLD.camera.lookAt(new THREE.Vector3(0,2,0) );

    $WORLD.clock = new THREE.Clock();
    $WORLD.controls={
        getPosition: function(){
            return $WORLD.camera.position;
        }
    };

    $WORLD.textureLoader = new THREE.TextureLoader();

    $WORLD.ambientLight = new THREE.AmbientLight(0xffffff,1);
    $WORLD.scene.add($WORLD.ambientLight);

    $WORLD.scene.fog = new THREE.Fog(0xffffff, 5, ($WORLD.distance - $WORLD.distance / 4));
    $WORLD.renderer.setClearColor($WORLD.scene.fog.color, 1);

    window.addEventListener('resize', onWindowResize, false);
    THREE.Loader.Handlers.add(/\.dds$/i, new THREE.DDSLoader());
    fSuc();
};

$WORLD.showStats = function() {
    if (!($WORLD.stats)) {
```

```
        $WORLD.stats = new Stats();
        $WORLD.stats.setMode(0);
        document.body.appendChild($WORLD.stats.domElement);
        $WORLD.addToListUpdate($WORLD.stats);
    };
};

$WORLD.startAnimation = function () {
    $WORLD.animate();
};

$WORLD.pauseAnimation = function () {
    window.cancelAnimationFrame( $WORLD.idAnim );
};

$WORLD.addToListUpdate = function (obj) {
    $WORLD._objUpdate.push(obj);
};

$WORLD.animate = function () {
    $WORLD.idAnim = requestAnimationFrame($WORLD.animate);
    var delta = $WORLD.clock.getDelta();
    for (var i = 0; i < $WORLD._objUpdate.length; i++) {
        $WORLD._objUpdate[i].update(delta);
    };
    $WORLD.renderer.render($WORLD.scene, $WORLD.camera);
};

function onWindowResize() {
    $WORLD.camera.aspect = window.innerWidth / window.innerHeight;
    $WORLD.camera.updateProjectionMatrix();
    $WORLD.renderer.setSize(window.innerWidth, window.innerHeight);
}
```

Creating the base ground (ground_v01.js)

Continuing with the example, let us focus on the file *ground_v01.js* where we've defined the method *$WORLD.drawGround* which creates the ground.

The simplest technique to create the base ground is by drawing a plane with a texture that is repeated endlessly. Later we'll see more advanced techniques. To create the plane, we used *THREE.PlaneBufferGeometry (x, z)* instead of using *THREE.PlaneGeometry,* since this class benefits from cache and additional optimizations included in *WebGL.* We've activated the reception of shadows in the plane (*reveiveShadows*), so that the characters and objects cast shadows on the ground.

In the property ***$WORLD.map*** we specify what world map should be like. To represent the map there are numerous techniques, such as creating a matrix of N x M and indicating which items there are in each cell. In this case, we define it using the *JSON* format. This format is very similar to how we define objects in JavaScript, but it has some limitations: the data type is limited and the properties must always be between (''), because the chains do not accept single quotation marks (') as delimiters.

For now, we'll specify what the ground should be like.

```
$WORLD.map = {
    "x":256,
    "z":256,
    "ground":{
        "type":"basic",
        "texture":"../data/graphics/textures/terrain/grassl.jpg",
        "resX":2,
        "resY":2
    }
};
```

To begin, we are going to specify the limits of *x* and *z* so that the camera or the player cannot leave this enclosure, in this case a square of 256x256. In the property *ground* we define the texture to be used and after how many units this texture must be repeated (*resX* and *resY*). We've added the property *type* to specify the technique we use to create the ground, so that in future examples we may give other values.

The plane size should be at least the width and height of the map plus the distance at which we can see objects. In other words: *width=width of map + 2.25 * distance vision*. We multiply it by *2.25* to leave a safety margin in case the algorithm that controls the limits allows deviations. For example, the control that moves the camera along a curve, as we've programmed, can generate curves slightly out of the limit.

To position the plane, we've taken into account that the part where we can move, starts at position *(0,0,0)*.

Let us look at the function code.

```
$WORLD.drawGround = function () {
    var map = $WORLD.map;
    var groundTexture = $WORLD.textureLoader.load(map.ground.texture);
    var x = $WORLD.distance * 2.25 + map.x;
    var z = $WORLD.distance * 2.25 + map.z;
    groundTexture.wrapS = groundTexture.wrapT = THREE.RepeatWrapping;
    groundTexture.repeat.set(x / 2, z / 2);
```

```
    groundTexture.anisotropy = 16;
    var groundMaterial = new THREE.MeshLambertMaterial(
      { color: 0xffffff, map: groundTexture }
    );
    var mesh = new THREE.Mesh(new THREE.PlaneBufferGeometry(x, z), groundMaterial);
    mesh.position.y = 0;
    mesh.position.x = map.x / 2;
    mesh.position.z = map.z / 2;
    mesh.rotation.x = - Math.PI / 2;
    mesh.receiveShadow = true;
    $WORLD.scene.add(mesh);
}
```

In the next picture, we see the result of the ground created.

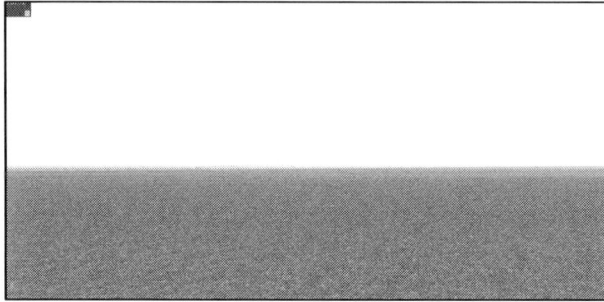

Fig. 4.7. Example of basic ground.

Moving an object along a set path (controls_path_v01.js)

Now that we have the ground we'll see how we've created the control that will move the camera along a set a path. You can see the code in the file *controls_path_v01.js*.

In fact, in games we'll find many occasions when we'll want to move an object along a predetermined route. For example, villagers can each be assigned to a route to go from shop to shop simulating the routine of going shopping. Or the camera can be moved along a predetermined route to create a cinematic scene.

For this, we have created a control to which we pass the object to move and the way to go. The path is an instance of the class *THREE.path*, which we used in the section where we talked about how to create flat figures with *THREE.Shape*.

If you open the file *07-ground.html*, you will see that we've used the class *THREE.CatmullRomCurve3* to define the path, which is an instance of the class *THREE.Path* and draws a curve from an array of points. From there, we create the instance of the controller and add it to the list of objects to be updated by the animation loop.

```
var path=new THREE.CatmullRomCurve3 ([
    new THREE.Vector3(5, 2, 50),

    ...

    new THREE.Vector3(50, 2, 33),
    new THREE.Vector3(5, 2, 50)])
$WORLD.controls = new $CONTROLS.PathControls ($WORLD.camera, path);
$WORLD.controls.showPath();
$WORLD.addToListUpdate ($WORLD.controls)
```

In the file *controls_path_v01.js* you can see the function **update,** which is called periodically and is responsible for moving the camera. It's useful to point out that we use the method **this.path.getPointAt (this._pos)** to get the point which we must move the camera, while we use the method *lookAt* to focus it towards the next point of the curve.

```
var $CONTROLS = $CONTROLS || {};

$CONTROLS.PathControls = function (object, path) {
        this.path=path;
        this._object=object;
        this._pos=0;
        this.velocity=1; // Units per second
        if (prop && prop.velocity){
            this.velocity=prop.velocity;
        }
        this._factor=this.velocity/this.path.getLength();
};

$CONTROLS.PathControls.prototype.update = function ( delta ) {
        this._object.position.copy(this.path.getPointAt(this._pos));
        this._pos += (this._factor * delta);
        if (this._pos > 1) {this._pos = 0;};
        this._object.lookAt(this.path.getPointAt(this._pos));
}

$CONTROLS.PathControls.prototype.showPath = function ( ) {
        var geometry = new THREE.Geometry();
        var points = this.path.getPoints(50);

        var material = new THREE.LineBasicMaterial({
            color: 0xff00f0
        });
        geometry.vertices = points;
        var line = new THREE.Line(geometry, material);
        line.position.set(0,-1.75,0)
        $WORLD.scene.add(line);
```

```
}

$CONTROLS.PathControls.prototype.getPosition = function ( ) {
        return this._object.position;
}
```

CREATING A SKY

Now that we have the ground to walk on we'll see different techniques on how to create a realistic sky. To do so we'll explore three methods:

- Creating the sky with a cube that surrounds the scene. Each of the six faces of the cube will be textured with a different image.
- Using a sphere instead of a cube with a wraparound graphic texture.
- Creating it using a sphere, but instead of using an image as texture, we'll use a gradient of colours.

Creating the sky with a cube (Skybox)

The simplest and most frequently used way of creating a sky in videogames is through a cube with a different image for each side. Each image represents a piece of sky. On the internet, you can find many examples of images already prepared for this kind of sky.

We've created an example, which can be accessed on the following link: https://www.thefiveplanets.org/b01/c04/08-skybox.html

The example stems from the code that we used to illustrate the creation of the basic ground. We've included the property "*sky*" to facilitate the creation of the cubic sky in our variable *$WORLD.map*. The property defines the 6 basic textures, as shown in the code below.

```
$WORLD.map = {
  ...
  "sky": {
    "type":"skybox",
    "colorAmbient" : "rgb(90, 90, 90)",
    "intensityAmbient" : 0.5,
    "sunlightcolor" : "rgb(255, 255, 255)",
    "sunlightposition": {"x":10, "y":20, "z":0},
    "sunlightintensity" : 1,
    "texture": ["../data/graphics/textures/skyboxes/night/px.jpg",
        "../data/graphics/textures/skyboxes/night/nx.jpg",
        "../data/graphics/textures/skyboxes/night/py.jpg",
        "../data/graphics/textures/skyboxes/night/ny.jpg",
        "../data/graphics/textures/skyboxes/night/pz.jpg",
        "../data/graphics/textures/skyboxes/night/nz.jpg"
    ],
    "fogColor": "rgb(14, 16, 16)",
    "fogNear":0,
    "fogFar":28
  }
```

};

The way the light and casting of shadows are affected is closely related to the sky and position the sun or the moon is in. Therefore, we've also specified the properties to create an ambient light (*colorAmbient* and *IntensityAmbient*) and a directional light with the ability to cast shadows (*sunlightcolor, sunlightposition*y *sunlightintensity*).

We've also added properties to create fog (*fogColor, fogNear* and *fogFar*). The colour of the fog should be similar to the texture on the line of the horizon. In this way, we can ensure that distant objects fade in to the background and disappear, preventing objects suddenly disappearing as they go out of the viewing range. In the example, we've used a night sky, so that the fog colour is a very dark grey in order to simulate shadows of the night.

The six textures are specified with the order marked by *px, nx, py, ny, pz, nz* that we see together in the next picture.

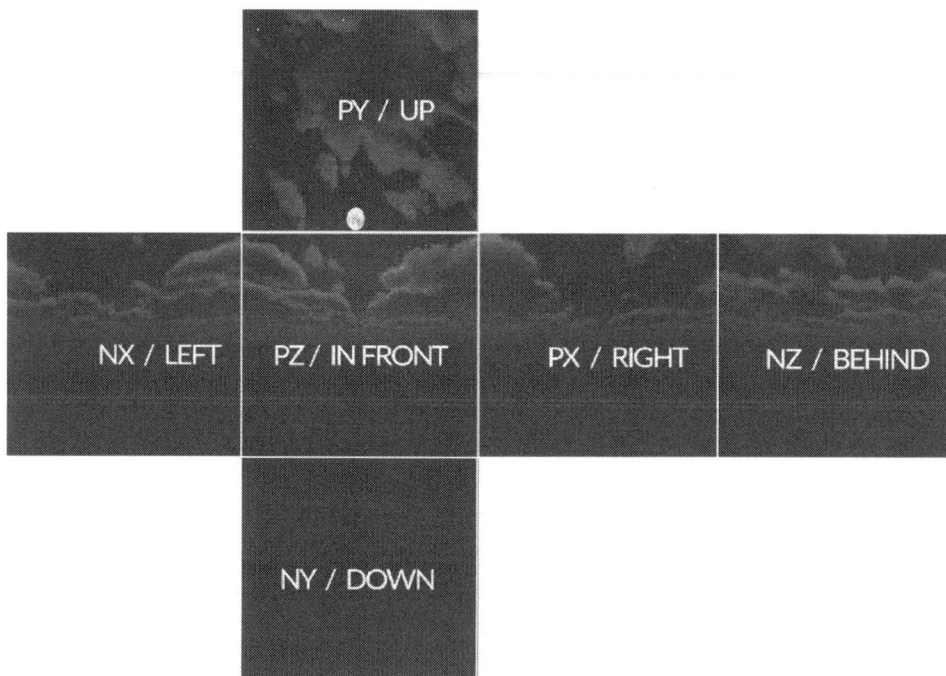

Fig. 4.8. Example of the 6 textures, with the position they will occupy in the cube.

All the logic to draw the sky, fog and lights has been added in a new file *sky_v01.js,* inside the folder *core\world*. The function that draws the cube is as follows:

```
$WORLD.drawSkybox=function (sky){
        var cubemap = new THREE.CubeTextureLoader().load( sky.texture );
        cubemap.format = THREE.RGBFormat;
```

```
var shader = THREE.ShaderLib['cube'];
shader.uniforms['tCube'].value = cubemap;

var skyBoxMaterial = new THREE.ShaderMaterial( {
fragmentShader: shader.fragmentShader,
vertexShader: shader.vertexShader,
uniforms: shader.uniforms,
depthWrite: false,
side: THREE.BackSide
});

var distance=($WORLD.distance*2-20);
var c = Math.pow ((distance*distance)/2,0.5);
var skyBox = new THREE.Mesh( new THREE.BoxGeometry(c, c, c), skyBoxMaterial);
$WORLD.scene.add(skyBox);
 $WORLD.sky.skyBox = skyBox;
};
```

Firstly, we load six textures. *Three.js* includes a class that allows simultaneous reading: ***new THREE.CubeTextureLoader().load(sky.texture)***.

We can create the material now that the textures are in the memory. We've used the classes *THREE.SharderMaterial* and *THREE.ShaderLib['cube']* to create a better effect in the cube. The use of *sharders* is beyond the scope of this book, so we'll look at it later.

Secondly, we create the cube. For the size of the sides we've created a mathematical formula with the viewing distance. The formula ensures that the cube will be in the viewable area, but with a maximum size, if we are located in the centre. We've set a margin of 20 units to ensure that the sky will remain visible if we are not exactly in the centre, but very close to it.

If we ran the example now we would find a problem. When moving the camera towards one edge of the sky, the front image would get bigger, while the rear face would cease to be visible. The solution is to link the centre of the cube to the position of the camera so that the whole sky moves together with the camera.

So now there would be no problems with the edges, because we'll never reach them. But all is not so simple when we jump or move upwards because the sky would also rise, moving itself towards the horizon. Therefore, the solution is not to move the sky up, and to limit the height to which the camera can rise.

To move the sky, I've defined the object *$WORLD.sky* with the function *update* to synchronize the movement of the sky with the camera (player in our case, this being a first-person game). Finally, I add the object code (*$WORLD.sky*) to update the list.

```
$WORLD.sky= {
        update:function(delta){
                var p = $WORLD.controls.getPosition();
                $WORLD.sky.skyBox.position.set(p.x, 0,  p.z);
        }
};

$WORLD.drawSky = function () {

        ...
        $WORLD.addToListUpdate ($WORLD.sky);
};
```

The last part of the code that we need to analyse is the creation of lights, the casting of shadows and the creation of fog. All this is also performed with the method *$WORLD.drawSky*.

```
$WORLD.drawSky = function () {
  var sky = $WORLD.map.sky;
  if (sky.type=="skybox"){
      $WORLD.drawSkybox(sky);
  } else if (sky.type=="skysphere" && sky.texture!="") {
      $WORLD.drawSkysphere(sky);
  } else {
      $WORLD.drawSkysphereNoImg(sky);
        }
  // CREATING THE AMBIENT LIGHT
  $WORLD.ambientLight.color = new THREE.Color(sky.colorAmbient);
  $WORLD.ambientLight.intensity = sky.intensityAmbient;

  // CREATE THE SUNLIGHT
  var light = new THREE.DirectionalLight(sky.sunlightcolor, sky.sunlightintensity);
  light.castShadow = true;
  light.shadow.mapSize.width = 2 * 512;
  light.shadow.mapSize.height = 2 * 512;
  light.shadow.camera.near = 0;
  light.shadow.camera.far = 50; // HEIGHT OF THE CUBE

  // FROM THE CENTRAL POINT INDICATE THE SQUARE
  light.shadow.camera.top = 25; //X
  light.shadow.camera.right = 25;
  light.shadow.camera.left = -25;
  light.shadow.camera.bottom = -25;
```

```
light.shadow.camera.visible = true;
$WORLD.sky.skyBox.add(light);

light.position.set(sky.sunlightposition.x, sky.sunlightposition.y, sky.sunlightposition.z);
light.target = $WORLD.sky.skyBox;

$WORLD.scene.fog.near = sky.fogNear;
if (sky.fogFar > 0 && ($WORLD.distance - $WORLD.distance / 4) > sky.fogFar) {
    $WORLD.scene.fog.far = sky.fogFar;
}
$WORLD.scene.fog.color = new THREE.Color(sky.fogColor);
$WORLD.renderer.setClearColor($WORLD.scene.fog.color, 1);

$WORLD.addToListUpdate ($WORLD.sky);
};
```

If we analyse the function code, we see that we change the intensity and colour of the ambient light and create a directional light. In the directional light, we specify a cube which has a height of 50 and a base of 25x25, which we cast shadows. The only unusual thing is that we do not add light to the scene, but add it to the cube and from the position of the light we focus it toward the centre of the cube. When we move sky that is linked to the camera we move the directional light at the same time with this technique. Thus, the objects around the camera will cast shadows, while the rest will stop casting them. By forfeiting the casting of distant shadows, we obtain much better performance.

When you run the example the result will be very similar to the image below.

Fig. 4.9. Example of cubic sky when running the code.

Creating a sky with a sphere (Skydome)

This technique is very similar to the previous one, but we use a sphere instead of using a cube. In this case, we only need one image to cover the inside of the sphere.

Creating sky texture manually can be a complex task. The image must be adjusted so that the edges fit together, in addition to moulding it to the sphere. Later we'll see how to create textures using programs like *Blender*. On the internet, you can find many images already prepared for use. In this case, we used the following texture.

Fig. 4.10. Texture prepared for skydome.

To illustrate this technique, we've created an example that you can access via the following link: https://www.thefiveplanets.org/b01/c04/09-skydome.html. The example that we use is the same as above, so we'll only outline the points that have changed.

In the main file (*10-skydome.html*) we've changed the property *$WORLD.map* to specify the technique to use, the texture and colour of light and density and colour of the fog. In this example, we create a sunny day, not a night sky as in the previous example.

```
$WORLD.map = {
        ...
     "sky": {
             "type":"skysphere",
             "colorAmbient" : "rgb(90, 90, 90)",
             "intensityAmbient" : 0.5,
             "sunlightcolor" : "rgb(255, 255, 255)",
             "sunlightposition": {"x":10, "y":20, "z":0},
             "sunlightintensity" : 1,
             "texture":"../data/graphics/textures/sky/skydome.jpg",
             "fogColor": "rgb(255, 255, 255)",
             "fogNear":6,
```

```
                    "fogFar":70
        }
};
```

In the file ***core/world/sky_v01.js*** we've defined the method $WORLD.*drawSkysphere* to draw the sphere and apply the texture.

```
$WORLD.drawSkysphere=function (sky){
    var skyTexture = $WORLD.textureLoader.load(sky.texture);
    var geometry = new THREE.SphereGeometry($WORLD.distance - 10, 30, 20);

    var uniforms = {
        texture: { type: 't', value: skyTexture }
    };
    var material = new THREE.ShaderMaterial({
        uniforms: uniforms,
        vertexShader: "varying vec2 vUV;" +
        "\n" +
        "void main() {  " +
        "  vUV = uv;" +
        "  vec4 pos = vec4(position, 1.0);" +
        "  gl_Position = projectionMatrix * modelViewMatrix * pos;" +
        "}",
        fragmentShader: "uniform sampler2D texture;" +
        "varying vec2 vUV;" +
        "" +
        "  void main() {" +
        "    vec4 sample = texture2D(texture, vUV);" +
        "    gl_FragColor = vec4(sample.xyz, sample.w);" +
        "  }"
    });

    var skyBox = new THREE.Mesh(geometry, material);
    skyBox.scale.set(-1, 1, 1);
    skyBox.rotation.order = 'XZY';
    skyBox.renderDepth = $WORLD.distance;
    $WORLD.scene.add(skyBox);
    $WORLD.sky.skyBox = skyBox;
};
```

Firstly, we load the texture, which in this case is much simpler because there is only one image. Then we create the geometry of the sphere. Knowing that the camera will always be in the centre of the sphere, the size is much easier to calculate, since the radius corresponds to the range of vision. As in the previous case, we take 10 points from each side to provide a safe distance and to prevent the sky from disappearing.

With the texture and geometry created, it only remains to create the material. In the example, we've reused *THREE.SharderMaterial* to achieve a better result. You may notice, when creating the material, we give it two properties *vertexSharder* and *fragmentSharder*. The *sharders* are pieces of code written in C++, which are executed very quickly.

The remaining code is the same as in the previous example, the sphere and the lights will move along with the camera and only the nearby objects will cast shadows.

Fig. 4.11. Example of spherical sky textured to run the code.

Creating a sky with a sphere and a gradient of colours

Sometimes, representing an empty sky is enough. In this case, we do not need an additional image to construct the sky. Instead we can play with colours, fading, and add some detail like a sphere to represent the sun or the moon.

Based on the example of the textured sphere, I've changed it and I created a very simple example. We simply create an area that will surround everything, in which we specify two colours for the fading. You can access the code via the following link:

https://www.thefiveplanets.org/b01/c04/10-skyshpere-noimg.html

In the main file (*10-skyshpere-noimg.html*) we simply change the way we describe the sky. In this case, I've left the property ***texture*** blank to specify that we do not want to load an image and have added two new properties (***topColor***, ***bottomColor***) to specify the fading of colours.

```
$WORLD.map = {
    ...
    "sky": {
        "type":"skysphere",
        "colorAmbient" : "rgb(90, 90, 90)",
        "intensityAmbient" : 0.5,
```

```
        "sunlightcolor" : "rgb(255, 255, 255)",
        "sunlightposition": {"x":10, "y":20, "z":0},
        "sunlightintensity" : 1,
        "texture":"",
        "topColor": 0x0055ff,
        "bottomColor": 0xffffff,
        "fogColor": 0xffffff,
        "fogNear":6,
        "fogFar":50
    }
};
```

Like the previous example, I did this with a *sharder*, a small program in C++, which I will explain more about later.

```
$WORLD.drawSkysphereNoImg=function (sky){

        var vertexShader = "varying vec3 vWorldPosition;"+
        " "+
        "void main() {"+
        "   vec4 worldPosition = modelMatrix * vec4( position, 1.0 );"+
        "   vWorldPosition = worldPosition.xyz;"+ //xyz
        " "+
        "   gl_Position = projectionMatrix * modelViewMatrix * vec4( position, 1.0 );"+
        "}";

        var fragmentShader = "uniform vec3 topColor;"+
        "uniform vec3 bottomColor;"+
        "uniform float offset;"+
        "uniform float exponent;"+
        " "+
        "varying vec3 vWorldPosition;"+
        " "+
        "void main() {"+
        "   float h = normalize( vWorldPosition + offset ).y;"+
        "   gl_FragColor = vec4( mix( bottomColor, topColor, max( pow( h, exponent ), 0.0 ) ), 1.0 );"+
        "}";

        var uniforms = {
            topColor: {type: "c", value: new THREE.Color(sky.topColor)}, bottomColor: {type: "c", value: new
THREE.Color(sky.bottomColor)},
            offset: {type: "f", value: 0}, exponent: {type: "f", value: 0.5}
        }
        var skyMaterial = new THREE.ShaderMaterial({vertexShader: vertexShader, fragmentShader:
fragmentShader, uniforms: uniforms, side: THREE.BackSide, fog: false});
```

```
                    var skyBox = new THREE.Mesh( new THREE.SphereGeometry($WORLD.distance - 10, 30, 20),
skyMaterial);

    skyBox.rotation.order = 'XZY';
    skyBox.renderDepth = $WORLD.distance;

    $WORLD.scene.add(skyBox);
    $WORLD.sky.skyBox = skyBox;
}
```

The rest of the code is the same as it is in the previous example. In the next picture, you can see the result.

Fig. 4.12. Example of spherical sky without texture.

CREATING VEGETATION AND NATURAL ELEMENTS

We need to include grass, flowers and trees in a realistic manner to simulate an idyllic nature scene realistically. To do this, we must be able to cover large areas of land with vegetation, without monopolizing the GPU. We must even be able to increase the realism, creating undulations, which simulate the effect of wind.

For trees, we can consider creating 3D models, but due to the extent of the area to cover they should be made with very few polygons.

Unfortunately, creating a detailed model of grass with individual blades is not viable, because the number of polygons required to create a single meadow would be too great and would not be viewable in real time with the hardware graphics currently available. So, we must build a simple and useful alternative that meets the following conditions:

- Many blades of grass should be represented by very few polygons.
- The grass should appear dense if viewed from different lines of sight.

Next, we will see different techniques to create grass and flowers that meet these conditions. Some of them also can be used to represent trees.

Using THREE.Sprite to create grass and trees

One way to create grass is to use *Sprites*. *Sprites* are flat images that are added to the scene and always have the same orientation, no matter how they are viewed. They are useful for placing the names of the characters on their heads so that they are always visible, regardless of their location, for example. They are also useful for simulating atmospheric effects, such as snowflakes, which we could represent by an image with a transparent background. We can also use *THREE.Sprite* for the user interface.

In this case, they are very useful to represent grass, as using detailed 3D objects is not viable due to performance limitations. The way to represent grass is with a still image of a shrub or several of them, with a transparent background, and randomly distribute them around the scene.

The problem is that this will only work as long as we place the camera close to the ground and focus it on the horizon, without turning it vertically, only horizontally. The good news is that we achieve optimal results in for a first-person game, in which the camera always points forward.

This technique is perfect for distant objects, which will never be reached, because we can create a dense forest without affecting performance excessively. It's also optimal for the grass close by, as they are small images so the distortions produced by turning the camera are less obvious.

Fig. 4.13. Example of grass created from sprites.

Click here to see an example of this technique: https://www.thefiveplanets.org/b01/c04/11-vegetation.html. In the example, we've also added the creation of trees with the same principle. The previous image shows the final result of the example.

If we analyse the code in the main file (*11 vegetation.html*), we see that we've added a new file JavaScript "*nature_v01.js*" inside the folder "*core/world*". This file contains the logic to create the vegetation.

```
<script src="../core/world/nature_v01.js" defer></script>
```

We've also included a new property (*nature*) within the definition of the map, to specify what images we use for vegetation and the areas we want to cover. Each zone will be covered randomly with the specified images.

Basically, we define patterns with the property "*patterns*". Each pattern specifies the repetition frequency of Sprites and the list of images with their size, *width* and *height*. In the example, we've defined two. Firstly "*bushes*" which contains images of the bushes and a repetition rate of 5 units of distance. Secondly "*forest*", with images of trees, seven to be precise, and a lesser repetition frequency (one tree every ten units of distance).

With the property "*zones*" we specify the areas covered with vegetation. We mark the area of each zone with a rectangle (*minX, MinZ, maxZ, maxX*), and this zone uses one of the patterns that we've defined. In the example, we use two overlapping areas, one for the trees and another for the bushes.

```
$WORLD.map = {
  ...
  "nature": {
    "type":"basic",
    "patterns": {
      "bushes":{
        "freqX":5,
        "freqZ":5,
        "elements":[
          {"object":"../data/graphics/textures/vegetation/grass.png","width":1.5," height":1.5},
          {"object":"../data/graphics/textures/vegetation/struik.png","width":1.5," height":1.5}
        ]
      },
      "forest":{
        "freqX":10,
        "freqZ":10,
        "elements":[
          {"object":"../data/graphics/textures/vegetation/tree01.png"," width ":8.75,"height ":8.91},
          {"object":"../data/graphics/textures/vegetation/tree02.png","width ":10,"height ":9.84},
```

```
                    {"object":"../data/graphics/textures/vegetation/tree03.png","width ":9.59,"y":8.65},
                    {"object":"../data/graphics/textures/vegetation/tree04.png","width ":6.1,"height ":8.65},
                    {"object":"../data/graphics/textures/vegetation/tree05.png","width ":10,"height ":7.66},
                    {"object":"../data/graphics/textures/vegetation/tree06.png","width ":8.94,"height ":13.9},
                    {"object":"../data/graphics/textures/vegetation/tree07.png","width ":10.2,"height ":14.53}
                ]
            }
        },
        "zones": [
            {"pattern":"forest","minX":-30,"minZ":-30,"maxZ":150,"maxX":150},
            {"pattern":"bushes","minX":-10,"minZ":-30,"maxZ":140,"maxX":140},
        ]
    } ...
```

Finally, in the function that initializes the environment, we add a call to $WORLD.drawNature(), which is responsible for adding nature to the scene. We've defined this function in the file *nature_v01.js* that we included at the beginning.

```
$WORLD.init3D({}, function () {
    ...
    $WORLD.drawSky();
    $WORLD.drawNature();
    ...
};
```

If you open the file *nature_v01.js* you will see the function code ***drawNature***, which is composed of two parts. In the first part, we go through the list of patterns and we create the *Sprites* with textures of trees and bushes, loading them in the memory. In the second part, we go over the zones and randomly clone the *Sprites* and add them to the scene, and this gradually covers the area. The result, therefore, will be a different forest every time we generate the scene.

```
$WORLD.drawNature = function () {
    var nat=$WORLD.map.nature;
    //PART ONE - LOADING ALL SPRITES IN MEMORY
    var list=Object.keys(nat.patterns);
    for (var i=0;i<list.length;i++) {
        var pat=nat.patterns[list[i]];
        for (var n=0;n<pat.elements.length;n++) {
            var el=pat.elements[n];
            var mat = new THREE.SpriteMaterial( { map: $WORLD.textureLoader.load(el.object),
useScreenCoordinates: false, transparent: true,fog:true} );
            var obj = new THREE.Sprite(mat);
            obj.scale.y=el.height;
            obj.scale.x=el.width;
            el._sprite = obj;
```

```
        }
    }
    // FOR EVERY AREA ADD TREES
    for (var j=0;j<nat.zones.length;j++) {
        var zon=nat.zones[j];
        var pat=nat.patterns[zon.pattern];
        for (var x=zon.minX;x<zon.maxX-pat.freqX;x+=pat.freqX) {
            for (var z=zon.minZ;z<zon.maxZ-pat.freqZ;z+=pat.freqZ) {
                var i=Math.round(Math.random()*(pat.elements.length-1));
                var el=pat.elements[i];
                var obj2=el._sprite.clone();
                obj2.position.set(x+(Math.random()*pat.freqX), el. height /2-0.05, z+(Math.random()*pat.freqZ));
                $WORLD.scene.add(obj2);
            }
        }
    }
};
```

Creating grass using planes

Another technique that we could employ, which is like the previous one, would be using planes, with the texture of the grass being repeated, as shown in the picture below.

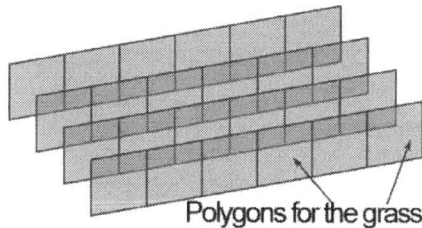

Polygons for the grass

Fig. 4.14. Example of bad distribution of grass.

Since the user can freely navigate through the scene, a similar construction to that shown in *figure 4.14* would be insufficient to produce a convincing effect. A linear configuration of grass planes would be easily recognizable if someone was positioned perpendicular to the direction of the planes. In these cases, the grass would be very thin or even disappear. Such distribution should only be considered when the camera moves automatically or for distant and unreachable meadows.

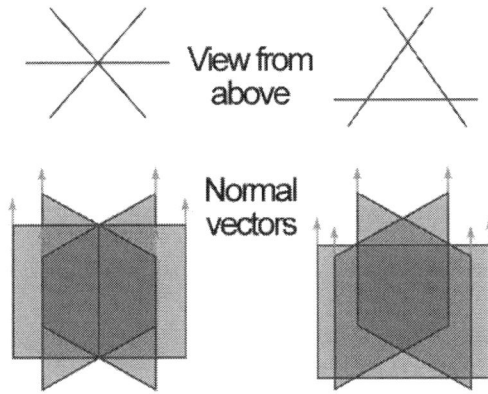

Fig. 4.15 Example of possible distribution of grass.

To ensure good visual quality regardless of the line of sight, we must cross the planes of grass. Using star-shaped configurations, as shown in *figure 4.15*, is very useful as they are displayed correctly from any angle. In the two possible distributions, we used three intersecting planes.

We need to make sure the planes are visible on both sides and that they accept a transparent texture. We've already used this technique in an earlier example, in which we represented a simple shrub to illustrate the operation of transparency. You can see the example here: https://www.thefiveplanets.org/b01/c03/19-transparent-texture.html.

Now we only need to improve the algorithm and clone the object we've made following the pattern of the next image. This is how we'll have a beautiful meadow visible from any angle.

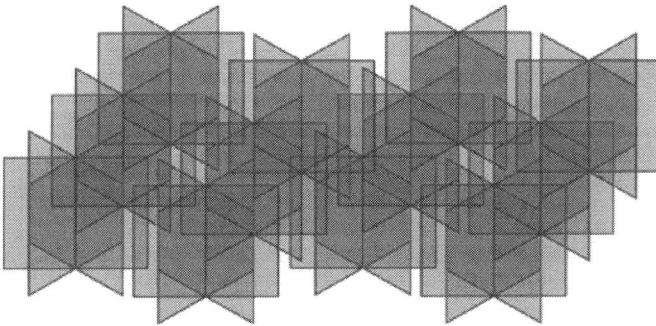

Fig. 4.16. Example of a grass distribution pattern.

You can see a complete example in which we use this technique here: https://www.thefiveplanets.org/b01/c04/12-vegetation-planes.html

Fig. 4.17. Example of the final distribution of grass.

CREATING THE GAME MAP

Now that we know how to create the terrain, vegetation and beautiful skies, it's time to start adding castles, villager huts treasure chests, etc. To do this we'll focus only on the modular technique.

By using this technique, we design individual objects, made to fit together instead of designing the whole the map with a *3D* tool, which would generate an object, which is very costly to load. For example, to create a castle, we can use parts of a wall and some models of the towers that we'll be duplicating on the map. We'll do the same with houses, and will have a few basic models that we'll be repeating, sometimes altering the scale, rotation and other basic properties to make them appear as if they were different models. As we are using web technology it's convenient to work with objects with few vectors and textures, and if possible to take advantage of reusing different objects.

You can o view and download the complete example via the following link: https://www.thefiveplanets.org/b01/c04/13-map.html.

The first step is to create the list of model-templates (*templates*), in which we specify the file of the *3D* model to upload and format for each item, as well as other properties that we'll define when we need them.

A first version could be as follows:

```
$RG.templates={
        "castle_wall_a": {"model" : "../data/models/castle/wall_a.obj"},
        "castle_wall_b": {"model" : "../data/models/castle/wall_b.obj"},
        "castle_wall_c": {"model" : "../data/models/castle/wall_c.obj"},
        "castle_gate_wall": {"model" : "../data/models/castle/gate_wall.obj"},
        "castle_metal_gate": {"model" : "../data/models/castle/metal_gate.obj"},
        "castle_tower1": {"model" : "../data/models/castle/tower1.obj"},
```

```
"castle_tower2": {"model" : "../data/models/castle/tower2.obj"},
"castle_tower3": {"model" : "../data/models/castle/tower3.obj"},
"house1": {"model": "../data/models/houses01/house1-01.obj"},
"house2": {"model": "../data/models/houses01/house1-02.obj"},
"house3": {"model": "../data/models/houses01/house1-03.obj"},
"house4": {"model": "../data/models/houses01/house1-04.obj"},
"well1": {"model": "../data/models/houses01/well-01.obj"},
"bench1": {"model": "../data/models/houses01/bench-01.obj"},
"house17": {"model": "../data/models/houses05/house5-01.obj"},
"house18": {"model": "../data/models/houses05/house5-02.obj"},
"house19": {"model": "../data/models/houses05/house5-03.obj"},
"house20": {"model": "../data/models/houses05/house5-04.obj"},
"house21": {"model": "../data/models/houses05/house5-05.obj"},
"house22": {"model": "../data/models/houses06/house6-01.obj"},
"house23": {"model": "../data/models/houses06/house6-02.obj"},
"house25": {"model": "../data/models/houses06/house6-03.obj"},

"tree07": {"model": "../data/graphics/textures/vegetation/tree07.png",
        "width":10.2, "height":14.53, "type":3}
}
```

You may observe that we've defined each template indicating a unique identifier (*castle_wall_a, castle_wall_b, castle_wall_c...*) and then the list of properties that define the object. In the list of properties, we must include at least the URL that points to the file containing the definition of the *3D* object. Optionally, we can specify additional properties that can helps us to specify the format of the object (*OBJ, DAE, JSON, SPRITE*), height, width, etc. These properties do not have to be the same on all templates. For example I've defined the property "*type*" to specify the format of the object: "0" for the format *.OBJ*, "1" for *.DAE*, "2" for *JSON*, "3" for *SPRITE*. In the example, I've only stated this specifically for the template "*tree07*" because we may assume that its value is 0 as it's not explicitly stated.

Over time we can add other properties like those that refer to physical laws, whether the object is solid or may be moved, its weight, if the object can be pushed and others properties, which are more specific to the game. For example, we can decide whether an object t is a magic potion and its effects on the player. These properties will always be generic for each type of template. For instance, we can specify the function of a potion. -it could be used to restore manna or to restore health. However, we can never do this with properties such as the position on the map, the number of loadings, etc. These properties are specified in the examples within the map.

Inside the folder "*core*" we've created a new folder "*entities*", that we've added the file ***template3D_v01.js* to**. In the code, we define the class *Template3D* that will handle the loading of the model in the memory, so we can then create duplicates.

We also define global function that will manage the load of the entire list of templates.

Here you can see the skeleton of the class *Template3D*:

```
var $RG = $RG || {};
$RG.templates={};
$RG.Types = $RG.Types || {};
$RG.Types.type3D = { "OBJ": 0, "DAE":1, "JSON":2, "SPRITE":3 };
.....
$RG.Template3D = function (id) {
    this.id = id;
    this._template=$RG.templates[id];
    this.isReady = false;
    this.mesh = null;
};
$RG.Template3D.prototype.load = function (oPars, fSuc, fFail) {
        var temp=this._template;
        if (!("type" in temp)) temp.type = $RG.Types.type3D.OBJ;
        if (temp.type == $RG.Types.type3D.OBJ) {
                this._loadOBJ(oPars,fSuc,fFail);
        } else if (temp.type == $RG.Types.type3D.DAE) {
                this._loadDAE(oPars,fSuc,fFail);
        } else if (temp.type == $RG.Types.type3D.JSON) {
                this._loadJSON(oPars,fSuc,fFail);
        } else if (temp.type == $RG.Types.type3D.SPRITE) {
                this._loadSPRITE(oPars,fSuc,fFail);
        } else {
                fFail();
        };
};
...
```

The class now has three properties: the identifier of the template (*id*), *mesh* to save the 3D model with its geometry and finally *isReady* to specify if it's loaded in the memory.

In order to create a new instance of the class *Template3D*, we use the identifier of the template as a parameter, so that we can access the properties of its definition.

The method *load* is responsible for reading the model and placing it in the memory. Note that the call is *ASYNCHRONOUS*, so we must give it as a parameter to the function which should be run once the loading is completed. The function *load* invokes *_loadOBJ, _loadDae, _loadJSON* and *_loadSPRITE,* depending on the format model. Note that I put an underscore before these names. This is because JavaScript does not easily allow us to define private properties or methods. We deal with private methods and properties whenever we use an _. That is, they should not be used outside the file and class definition.

Next I will display the code functions _loadOBJ and _loadSPRITE. Notice that I've not included either _loadDAE or _loadJSON because we'll not use models of the JSON or DAE type for the example. We'll do this at a later stage.

```
$RG.Template3D.prototype._loadOBJ = function (oPars,fSuc, fFail) {
    var $0 = this;
    var onProgress = function (xhr) {   };
    var onError = function (xhr) { if (fFail) { fFail($0); } };
    var mtlLoader = new THREE.MTLLoader();
    var pathArray = $0._template.model.split('/');
    var mP = '';
    for (var i = 0; i < pathArray.length-1; i++) {
        mP += pathArray[i];
        mP += "/";
    }
    var model = pathArray[pathArray.length - 1];
    mtlLoader.setPath(mP);
    model=model.substr(0,model.length - 4)
    mtlLoader.load(model + '.mtl', function (materials) {
        materials.preload();
        var objLoader = new THREE.OBJLoader();
        objLoader.setMaterials(materials);
        objLoader.setPath(mP);
        objLoader.load(model + '.obj', function (object) {
            object.traverse(function (child) {
                if (child instanceof THREE.Mesh) {
                    child.castShadow = true;
                }
            });
            $0.mesh = object;
            $0.mesh.castShadow = true;
            $0.isReady = true;
            if (fSuc) { fSuc($0); }

        }, onProgress, onError);

    }, onProgress, onError);
};


$RG.Template3D.prototype._loadSPRITE = function (oPars, fSuc, fFail) {
    var $0 = this;
    var onProgress = function (xhr) {   };
    var onError = function (xhr) { if (fFail) { fFail($0); } };
```

```
$WORLD.textureLoader.load($0._template.model, function (texture) {
        var mat = new THREE.SpriteMaterial( { map: texture, useScreenCoordinates: false, transparent:
true,fog:true} );
        var object =new THREE.Sprite(mat);
        object.scale.y=$0._template.height;
        object.scale.x=$0._template.width;
        $0.mesh = object;
        $0.isReady = true;
        fSuc($0.mesh);
   }, onProgress, onError);
};
```

Loading multiple non-animated models simultaneously

At this point we are ready to create the global method that loops through the list and loads the templates in the memory, so that they can be used subsequently in creating the map. The code is in the file ***template3D_v01.js***.

This method invokes the start of the game, every time we load a game or enter a new map. A first version of the code is as follows.

```
$RG.loadTemplates = function (fSuc, fFail, fProgress) {
        var i=0;
        var list=Object.keys($RG.templates);
        var _load = function () {
                if (list.length==i) {
                        fSuc();
                        return;
                }
                var ent=$RG.templates[list[i]].template3D=new $RG.Template3D(list[i]);
                if (fProgress) {fProgress(list[i],i+1,list.length)}
                i++;
                ent.load({},_load, fFail);
        }
        _load();
};
```

Note that loading models and images is asynchronous, so we've included three parameters in order to be able to specify what to do during and after loading the templates. The first parameter (*fSuc*) is the function to execute when downloading is completed, the second (*fFail*) is the function to handle errors and the third (*fProgress*) is the function of progress that will be invoked whenever an object is read. Remember that the method for handling errors is important in web development, because loading objects can generate a *timeout* error with a slow connection, for example. The function of progress (*fProgress*), will be useful to us in order to display a bar or animation indicating the progress in loading.

Cloning objects

Now that we've all the models-templates in the memory, we can create the map based on the elements that have already been created, like the ground, vegetation and sky, tailoring them to the needs of the map.

```
$WORLD.map = {
  "x":256,
  "z":256,
  "startPosX":126,
  "startPosZ":145,
  "ground": {
    "type":"basic",
    "texture":"../data/graphics/textures/terrain/grass1.jpg",
    "resX":2,
    "resY":2
  },
  "sky": {
    "type":"skysphere",
    "colorAmbient" : "rgb(90, 90, 90)",
    "intensityAmbient" : 0.5,
    "sunlightcolor" : "rgb(255, 255, 255)",
    "sunlightposition": {"x":10, "y":20, "z":0},
    "sunlightintensity" : 1,
    "texture":"../data/graphics/textures/sky/skydome.jpg",
    "fogColor": "rgb(225, 225, 225)",
    "fogNear":70,
    "fogFar":130
  },
  "nature": {
    "type":"basic",
    "patterns": {
      "bushes":{
        "freqX":5,
        "freqZ":5,
        "elements":[
          {"object":"../data/graphics/textures/vegetation/grass.png","width":1.5,"height":1.5},
          {"object":"../data/graphics/textures/vegetation/struik.png","width":1.5,"height":1.5}
        ]
      },
      "forest":{
        "freqX":10,
        "freqZ":10,
        "elements":[
          {"object":"../data/graphics/textures/vegetation/tree01.png","width":8.75,"height":8.91},
          {"object":"../data/graphics/textures/vegetation/tree02.png","width":10,"height":9.84},
```

```
                {"object":"../data/graphics/textures/vegetation/tree03.png","width":9.59,"height":8.65},
                {"object":"../data/graphics/textures/vegetation/tree04.png","width":6.1,"height":8.65},
                {"object":"../data/graphics/textures/vegetation/tree05.png","width":10,"height":7.66},
                {"object":"../data/graphics/textures/vegetation/tree06.png","width":8.94,"height":13.9},
                {"object":"../data/graphics/textures/vegetation/tree07.png","width":10.2,"height":14.53}
            ]
        },
        "hightTrees":{
            "freqX":12,
            "freqZ":12,
            "elements":[
                {"object":"../data/graphics/textures/vegetation/tree06.png","width":10,"height":20.68},
                {"object":"../data/graphics/textures/vegetation/tree07.png","width":12,"height":22.43}
            ]
        }


    },
    "zones": [
        {"pattern":"forest","minX":0,"minZ":50,"maxZ":260,"maxX":114},
        {"pattern":"bushes","minX":20,"minZ":50,"maxZ":260,"maxX":117},
        {"pattern":"hightTrees","minX":110,"minZ":40,"maxZ":110,"maxX":200},
        {"pattern":"bushes","minX":110,"minZ":80,"maxZ":113,"maxX":140},
        {"pattern":"hightTrees","minX":0,"minZ":217,"maxZ":280,"maxX":230}
    ]
},
"map3D": [
    { "template": "castle_wall_c", "x": 214, "z": 110, "rY": -90 , "coment":"Size X:120-230, z:110-215"},
    { "template": "castle_tower2", "x": 210, "z": 110 },
    { "template": "castle_wall_a", "x": 199, "z": 110, "rY": -90 },
    { "template": "castle_tower1", "x": 188, "z": 110, "rY": -90  },
    { "template": "castle_gate_wall", "x": 177, "z": 110, "rY": -90 },
    { "template": "castle_metal_gate", "x": 177, "z": 110, "rY": -90 },
    { "template": "castle_tower1", "x": 166, "z": 110, "rY": -90  },
    { "template": "castle_wall_a", "x": 155, "z": 110, "rY": -90  },
    { "template": "castle_tower2", "x": 143, "z": 110 },

    { "template": "castle_wall_c", "x": 120, "z": 129},
    { "template": "castle_tower1", "x": 120, "z": 134},
    { "template": "castle_gate_wall", "x": 120, "z": 145},
    { "template": "castle_metal_gate", "x": 120, "z": 145, "y":2.5},
    { "template": "castle_tower1", "x": 120, "z": 156},
    { "template": "castle_wall_b", "x": 120, "z": 173},
    { "template": "castle_tower3", "x": 120, "z": 192},
    { "template": "castle_wall_c", "x": 140, "z": 215, "rY": 90},

    { "template": "castle_tower2", "x": 144, "z": 215},
```

```
    { "template": "castle_wall_b", "x": 157, "z": 215, "rY": 90 },
    { "template": "castle_tower2", "x": 176, "z": 215},
    { "template": "castle_wall_b", "x": 190, "z": 215, "rY": 90 },
    { "template": "castle_tower2", "x": 210, "z": 215},
    { "template": "castle_wall_c", "x": 233, "z": 199, "rY": 180 },

    { "template": "castle_tower2", "x": 233, "z": 132},
    { "template": "castle_wall_b", "x": 233, "z": 150, "rY": 180 },
    { "template": "castle_tower2", "x": 233, "z": 165},
    { "template": "castle_wall_b", "x": 233, "z": 185, "rY": 180 },
    { "template": "castle_tower2", "x": 233, "z": 199},

    { "template": "house1", "x": 155, "z": 150, "rY": -25, "comment" : "houses01" },
    { "template": "well1", "x": 135, "z": 146, "rY": -45 },
    { "template": "bench1", "x": 145, "z": 153, "rY": -25 },
    { "template": "house22", "x": 134, "z": 130,"rY": 110 },
    { "template": "house23", "x": 150, "z": 125,"rY": 45 },
    { "template": "house4", "x": 170, "z": 132, "rY": -25},

    { "template": "house17", "x": 135, "z": 162, "rY": -100, "comment" : "houses05" },
    { "template": "house18", "x": 154, "z": 172,"rY": -45},
    { "template": "house19", "x": 170, "z": 170,"rY": -55 },
    { "template": "house20", "x": 174, "z": 155,"rY": -35 },
    { "template": "house21", "x": 178, "z": 142,"rY": 45 },

    { "template": "house22", "x": 133, "z": 180,"rY": 200, "comment" : "houses06" },
    { "template": "house3", "x": 148, "z": 190, "rY": -15 },
    { "template": "house2", "x": 168, "z": 190, "rY": 20 },
    { "template": "house25", "x": 185, "z": 190, "rY": -5 },

    { "template": "tree07", "x": 145, "z": 141 },
    { "template": "tree07", "x": 146, "z": 166 },
    { "template": "tree07", "x": 135, "z": 196 }
    ]
};
```

We've added the property *Map3D* to the object *$WORLD.map* which defines the map and the characteristics of the world, in which we define an *array* of the different elements that make up the map (the houses, walls, towers, etc.). For each element, we specify the *identifier* template we use and the position of the object on the *x-axis* and *z-axis*, and optionally the *y-axis*, as well as other properties that customize the appearance and behaviour of the object. For example, in this case I added a property to change the inclination (*rY*) of the object on the map. Another property could be that of indicating the actions to be executed after a customised event.

Inside the folder "*core/entities*" I've created the JavaScript file ***entity3D_v01.js***, which defines the class ***Entity3D***. This class, based on an item on the map, is responsible for searching for the templates, cloning the mesh and adding them to the scene in the position specified.

If we analyze the code we see that to create an instance of the Entity3D class we pass as parameter the element of the map with its properties (the template and position, among others). The method ***addToWorld***, searches the template-model in the list of templates *$RG.templates* and clones the *mesh* then adjusts the position of the cloned object and rotates it if necessary.

```
var $RG = $RG || {};
$RG.entities=[];

$RG.Entity3D = function (properties) {
    this.template=properties.template
    this.prop=properties;
    this.mesh=null;
    $RG.entities.push(this)
};

$RG.Entity3D.prototype.addToWorld = function () {
    var prop=this.prop;
    var templ=$RG.templates[prop.template];
    // Clone the 3D figure, position and rotate
    var mesh=templ.template3D.mesh.clone();
    var y=0;
    mesh.position.set(prop.x, ((prop.y)?prop.y:0), prop.z);
    if (!(prop.rY)) prop.rY=0;
    if (templ.type=3) {
        mesh.translateY(templ.height/2-0.05);
    };
    mesh.rotateY(prop.rY * Math.PI / 180);
    this.mesh=mesh;

    $WORLD.scene.add(mesh);
    return mesh;
};
```

Finally, in the main file (***13-map.html***), we add the loop which, once the templates are loaded in the memory, goes through the list *$WORLD.map.map3D*, creating *Entity3D* instances and call the function *addToWorld* to add the *mesh* to the scene.

Once the map is fully loaded we use the controller *$CONTROLS.PathControls* to move the camera around the map and to allow us to walk through the village and the forest.

```
$RG.loadTemplates( function() {
    for (var i=0;i<$WORLD.map.map3D.length;i++){
        var props=$WORLD.map.map3D[i];
        var ent=new $RG.Entity3D(props);
        ent.addToWorld();
    };

    var path=new THREE.CatmullRomCurve3([
        new THREE.Vector3(96, 2, 131),

        ...

    ]);
    $WORLD.controls = new $CONTROLS.PathControls ($WORLD.camera, path, {"velocity":3});
    $WORLD.addToListUpdate ($WORLD.controls);
    $WORLD.startAnimation();
});
```

The following images show how the example looks on the screen.

Fig. 4.18. Map view within the city.

Fig. 4.19. Map view from the outskirts of the city.

Creating a progress bar and a loading screen (SplashScreen)

Uploading models, textures and JavaScript libraries may take a while. It's therefore a good idea to create a progress bar, which will also prevent the player from thinking that the website is not loading, and will make them refrain from opening it. If we create a progress bar, then the user will see that the game is working and can see the waiting time.

Another important element is the loading screen (*splashScreen*), which is nothing more than a layer (*div*) covering the entire screen and is displayed above the rest of the elements. It's usually displayed with a background image of the application logo. This element has two purposes, firstly to hide the elements that make up the web page while they are being drawn and positioned, and on the other hand it also serves to display the logo or product name and create a brand image, which is important to build loyalty in our users.

From the above example, we'll create the loading screen (*splashScreen*). Once we create it, we'll add the logo, the progress bar and a text box on it to inform the user of the actions we are taking.

You can view and download the final version here:
https://www.thefiveplanets.org/b01/c04/14-map-loadingbar.html.

Fig. 4.20. Example of the progress bar..

We've added two nested layers (*div*) in the main file (***14-map-loading.html***) inside the *body*, which until now was empty.

```
<div id = "lyr_loading">
    <div id = "lyr_loading_background"></div>
    <div id = "lyr_loading_logo" class = "ui_logo"></div>
</div>
```

The layer (*lyr_loading*) will act as the loading screen (*splashScreen)*, which is composed of two layers: *lyr_loading_background, which* shows the background image that covers the entire screen. In our example, we've applied a filter to convert it to black and white, and when we load the application, we'll alter the background by adding colour. The other layer *(lyr_loading_logo)* will be used to display the application logo.

We've added the style file "***css\ui.cs***" to define the appearance of our graphical interface, where we'll be adding styles to create screens. throughout the examples.

```
#lyr_loading {
    position:absolute;
    top:0px;
    left:0px;
    width:100%;
    height:100%;
    overflow:hidden;
    z-index:100000;
    display: block;
    padding:0px;
    margin:0px;
```

```
}

#lyr_loading_background {
    position:absolute;
    top:0px;
    left:0px;
    width:100%;
    height:100%;
    overflow:hidden;
    background: url('../data/graphics/ui/loading/default.jpg') no-repeat center center fixed;
    background-size: cover;
    -webkit-filter: grayscale(100%);
    filter: grayscale(100%);
    transition:all ease-in-out 0.3s;
}

#lyr_loading_logo {
    bottom: 90px;
    position: absolute;
    left: calc(50% - 250px);
}

.ui_logo{
    background: url('../data/graphics/logo_big.png') no-repeat;
    background-size: contain;
    width: 500px;
    height: 200px;
}
```

If we analyse the styles, we see that the layers *lyr_loading* and *lyr_loading_background* are located in the position (0,0), occupying the whole width and height of the screen. With *"z-indez:100000"*, *lyr_loading* will always be above any element. In the layer with the background image we use *background-size:cover* to ensure that the entire screen is covered. Anyway, according to the image size, part of it will be hidden, so it might be necessary to use multiple images depending on the device that we open the application with and whether the format of the screen is in *landscape* or *portrait* mode.

To specify the progress of the loading of the models and the actions taken at the opening of the application, we've created a progress bar. The bar is built with two layers (*div*), superimposed on each other, using the two images in *figure 4.21*. The lower layer shows the image of the bar frame without any filling, while the top layer corresponds to the red fading colour. The trick is to only partially show the image of the filling, by playing with the *width* of the layer, which we calculate by multiplying the percentage of progress by the width of the image of the filling. On the bar, we've placed a layer which is overlaid to display a message with the text "Loading ...".

Fig. 4.21. Images to create the progress bar.

Unlike the loading screen, the layers of the bar are created by code. In this way, we can reuse the code to create other bars, such as experience, life or manna. The styles for the three layers that make up the bar have been included in the file ***ui.css*** and they are as follows.

```
.ui_loadingbar {
    background: url('../data/graphics/ui/misc/loading_bar_frame.png') no-repeat;
    position:absolute;
    width:701px;
    height:52px;
    bottom:30px;
    left: calc(50% - 350px);
}

.ui_loadingbar .ui_barfill {
    background: url('../data/graphics/ui/misc/loading_bar_fill.png') no-repeat;
    position:absolute;
    top:18px;
    left:16px;
    width:670px;
    max-width:670px;
    height:16px;
}

.ui_loadingbar .ui_text {
    position:absolute;
    top:18px;
    left:16px;
    width:670px;
    max-width:670px;
    height:16px;
    overflow:hidden;
    text-align:center;
    font-size:10px;
    padding:1px;
    text-transform: uppercase;
    color:#fff;
}
```

Now that we have the loading screen and progress bar ready for use, we can now create functions to show and hide the loading screen, or to move the progress indicator. The code for this is in a new file *"core/ ui/ui.js"*.

```
var $UI = $UI || {};

$UI.drawloading = function () {
    $UI.loading = new $UI.Loading("lyr_loading", { title: 'Loading...' });
}

//CLASE $UI.Loading
$UI.Loading = function (cld,oPars) {
    this.id = cld;
    this.vaule = 0;
    $('#' + cld).append('<div id="' + cld + '_loadbar" class="ui_loadingbar"><div id="' + cld + '_loadbarfill" class="ui_barfill" style="width:0px"></div><div class="ui_text">'+oPars.title+'</div></div>');
};
$UI.Loading.prototype.show = function () { $('#' + this.id).fadeIn("fast"); };
$UI.Loading.prototype.hide = function () { $('#' + this.id).fadeOut("slow"); };
$UI.Loading.prototype.setValue = function (nPor) {
    if (nPor < 0) (nPor = 0);
    if (nPor > 1) (nPor = 1);
    $('#' + this.id + '_loadbarfill').css('width', Math.round(nPor * 670));
    $('#' + this.id + '_background').css('-webkit-filter', 'grayscale(' + (100 - (nPor * 100)) + '%)');
    $('#' + this.id + '_background').css('filter', 'grayscale(' + (100 - (nPor * 100)) + '%)');
};
```

In the JavaScript file, we define the class *$UI.Loading* with three functions: *Show,* which shows the loading screen with the bar; *hide* to hide it and *setValue (nPercentage)* that, when given a value of 0 to 1, updates the progress bar and colours the background image.

The global function *$UI.drawloading* creates an instance of the class *$UI.Loading* and assigns it to the property *$UI.loading*. Thus, the instructions *$UI.loading.show()* and *$UI.loading.hide()* show or hide the loading screen.

As a last step, we've modified the main file (*14-map-loading.html*) to include references to the new files of styles and the JavaScript code.

```
<link rel="stylesheet" type="text/css" href="../core/ui/ui.js"/>
<link rel="stylesheet" type="text/css" href="../css/ui.css"/>
```

We've also modified the code to include instructions for managing the progress bar and the loading screen.

```
$(document).ready(function () {
    $UI.drawloading();
    $UI.loading.setValue(0);
    $UI.loading.show();
    $WORLD.distance = 130;
    $WORLD.init3D({}, function () {
        $UI.loading.setValue(0.05);//5%

        ...

        $RG.loadTemplates( function() {
            var elements=$WORLD.map.map3D.length;
            for (var i=0;i<elements;i++){
                var props=$WORLD.map.map3D[i];
                var ent=new $RG.Entity3D(props);
                ent.addToWorld();
                $UI.loading.setValue( ((i/elements)*0.20) +0.80);
            }
        },function () {
                // Handling errors..
        },function (template,i,elements) {
                // Update bar. Reserve 75% for the loading of the templates.
                $UI.loading.setValue( ((i/elements)*0.75) +0.05);
        });
    });
})
```

ADDING VILLAGERS AND CREATING THEIR DAILY ROUTINES

Now that we know how to create a map with static elements, we'll enhance it by incorporating living characters. Firstly, we will create a well-built group of villagers to populate our city. Each villager will have their own name and daily routine. By daily routine we mean doing activities like getting up, leaving home, visiting the cemetery, going to eat, work or sleep. To do this we'll write an early version of very basic artificial intelligence that will establish the routine of every villager, by indicating a list of points that they will pass through, which is like the style of games such as *"Elder Scrolls"*. This simple logic can be improved by including instructions to stop for a moment or by activating different animations depending on the action taken.

You can view and download the final version here:
https://www.thefiveplanets.org/b01/c04/15-map-villagers.html.

From the above example, the first step is to include a generic template for the villagers, as shown below. Notice that we've increased the properties. In addition to including the model and type (DAE, JSON, OBJ or SPRITE), we must specify that this is an animated object, and the algorithm used to implement the artificial intelligence (**"Ai": "Pathai"**). Likewise, we've included the properties *scale* and *rotate* to alter the model of the template, without editing with a 3D tool.

```
$RG.templates={
    ...
    "villager01": {
        "model": "../data/models/people/aldeano01.dae",
        "type":1, "animation":true,
        "ai":"PathAI",
        "scale":{"x":1.5,"y":1.5,"z":1.5},
        "rotate":{"x":-90,"y":0,"z":0}
    }
}
```

In the list of map elements (*$WORLD.map.map3D*) we can now add our villagers based on the template created. In the example, we've added three. For each one we specify their position as we did for the other elements of the map, but we've incorporated the properties *path*, *showPath* and *name*. The first two will be used by the artificial intelligence algorithm to move the villager around the map, generating movements which imitate daily routines. With *name,* we specify the name of the villager.

```
$WORLD.map = {
    "x":256,
    "z":256,
    ...
    "map3D": [
        { "template": "castle_wall_c", "x": 214, "z": 110, "rY": -90},
        ....
        { "template": "villager01", "x": 139, "z": 144,
"path":[[171,0,131],[164,0,130],[159,0,130],[156,0,134],[149,0,141],[145,0,145],[139,0,150],[129,0,149],[127,0,1
44],[133,0,140],[169,0,131],[140,0,138],[144,0,135],[145,0,131],[146,0,129],[147,0,128],[149,0,126],[148,0,128]
,[144,0,130],[142,0,126],[141,0,121],[149,0,117],[160,0,121],[136,0,129],[166,0,130],[169,0,131]],
"showPath":true, name:"Borat"},
        { "template": "villager01", "x": 140, "z": 145,
"path":[[135,0,133],[136,0,136],[131,0,142],[132,0,152],[141,0,152],[145,0,163],[144,0,173],[142,0,184],[138,0,190],[127,0,
191.5],[120.5,0,191.5],[120.5,0,159],[121,0,156],[128,0,156],[133,0,150],[132,0,143],[137,0,138],[136,0,134]],
"showPath":true, name:"Xena"},
        { "template": "villager01", "x": 140, "z": 145,
"path":[[135,0,179],[136,0,179],[140,0,177],[152,0,181],[156,0,185],[157,0,190],[160,0,194],[163,0,192],[167,0,190],[172,
0,189],[176,0,188],[179,0,190],[180,0,190],[183,0,190],[185,0,190]], "showPath":true, name:"Conan" }
    ]
};
```

We'll not change the JavaScript file "***core/entities/template3D_v01.js***", which is responsible for loading templates in the memory. If we open it, we see the function *_loadDAE* which loads templates with *3D* models of the *collada* type (*DAE*).

```
$RG.Template3D.prototype._loadDAE = function (oPars, fSuc, fFail) {
    var $0 = this;
    var temp =$0._template;
    var loader = new THREE.ColladaLoader();
    var onProgress = function (xhr) {   };
    var onError = function (xhr) { if (fFail) { fFail($0); } };
    loader.load(temp.model, function (collada) {
        var object = collada.scene;
        var mesh=null;
        object.traverse(function (child) {
            if (child instanceof THREE.Mesh) {
                child.castShadow = true;
                mesh=child;
            }
        });

        if (temp.scale) {
            mesh.scale.x = temp.scale.x;
            mesh.scale.y = temp.scale.y;
            mesh.scale.z = temp.scale.z;
        }
        if (temp.rotate) {
            if (temp.rotate.x) {
                mesh.rotateX (temp.rotate.x * Math.PI / 180);
            };
            if (temp.rotate.y) {
                mesh.rotateY (temp.rotate.y * Math.PI / 180);
            };
            if (temp.rotate.z) {
                mesh.rotateZ (temp.rotate.z * Math.PI / 180);
            };
        $0.mesh = object;
        $0.isReady = true;
        fSuc(mesh);
    }, onProgress, onError);
};
```

Cloning animated objects

Now that we have the templates-model loaded in memory we only need to clone them for each individual villager. If you remember, we created the file "*core/entities/entity3D_v01.js*" in which we defined the class *Entity3D* that was responsible for cloning and adding items to the scene. We'll create a new version of this file "*core/entities/entity3D_v02.js*", which will manage the new properties (*animation* and *ai*). The first (**animation**) specifies that the animation of the model should be activated. The second (**ai**) tells us the name of the class to implement the artificial intelligence. If you look at the code, if this property is present, then we create the class and add it to the update list.

```
var $RG = $RG || {};
$RG.entities=[];

$RG.Entity3D = function (properties) {
    this.template=properties.template
    this.prop=properties;
    this.mesh=null;
    $RG.entities.push(this)
}

$RG.Entity3D.prototype.addToWorld = function () {
    var prop=this.prop;
    var templ=$RG.templates[prop.template];

    //Clone the 3D figure, position and rotate
    var mesh=templ.template3D.mesh.clone();
    var y=0
    mesh.position.set(prop.x, ((prop.y)?prop.y:0), prop.z);
    if (!(prop.rY)) prop.rY=0;
    if (templ.type=3) {
        mesh.translateY(templ.height/2-0.05);
    }
    mesh.rotateY(prop.rY * Math.PI / 180);
    this.mesh=mesh;

    // Animate the object if they have an animation
    if (templ.animation) {
        mesh.traverse(function (child) {
            if (child instanceof THREE.SkinnedMesh) {
                var animation = new THREE.Animation(child, child.geometry.animation);
                animation.play();
            }
        })
    };

    // Apply artificial intelligence if defined
    if (templ.ai) {
        this.ai=new $AIS[templ.ai](this.mesh, this.prop);
```

```
        $WORLD.addToListUpdate (this.ai);
    }
    $WORLD.scene.add(mesh);
    return mesh;
};
```

Creating basic Artificial Intelligence through pre-established routes

Inside the folder "*core*" we've created the folder "*ai*", which we've include various classes in to give map objects intelligent behaviour. For the villagers, we've created the file "*core\ai\ai_path_v01.js*", which we add the class **$AIS.PathAI**. If we analyse the code will see that it's very simple and is like the one we used to move the camera along a specific path.

We instantiate the class by indicating the *mesh* and the properties of the map element. In the properties, we must specify at least the route (**path**). We can optionally add *showPath* to specify that the path to be displayed and the *velocity* to specify the distance in units per second that the villager covers. The path in this case is an *array* of points that the villager must cover. With these points, we draw a curve (*THREE.CatmullRomCurve3*) that will guide the movements of the character.

The function *$AIS.PathAI.prototype.update* is responsible for updating the villager's position over time, where delta is the amount of time in milliseconds that has passed since the last call.

```
var $AIS = $AIS || {};

$AIS.PathAI = function (object, prop) {
    var vecs=[];
    for (var i=0;i<prop.path.length;i++){
        vecs.push(new THREE.Vector3(prop.path[i][0], prop.path[i][1], prop.path[i][2]));
    };

    this.path=new THREE.CatmullRomCurve3(vecs);
    this._object=object;
    this._pos=0;
    this.velocity=1; // Units per second
    if (prop.velocity){
        this.velocity=prop.velocity;
    };

    this._factor=this.velocity/this.path.getLength();
    if (prop.showPath) {
        this.showPath();
    };
```

```
};

$AIS.PathAI.prototype.update = function ( delta ) {
    this._object.position.copy(this.path.getPointAt(this._pos));
    this._pos += (this._factor * delta);
    if (this._pos > 1) {this._pos = 0;};
    this._object.lookAt(this.path.getPointAt(this._pos));
};

$AIS.PathAI.prototype.showPath = function ( ) {
    var geometry = new THREE.Geometry();
    var points = this.path.getPoints(50);
    var material = new THREE.LineBasicMaterial({
        color: 0xff00f0
    });

    geometry.vertices = points;
    var line = new THREE.Line(geometry, material);
    line.position.set(0,0.25,0)
    $WORLD.scene.add(line);
};

$AIS.PathAI.prototype.getPosition = function ( ) {
    return this._object.position;
};
```

Now it's only necessary to include the script in the HTML main file (*15-map-villagers.html*), together with the new version of the class *entity3D* (*entity3D_v02.js*).

```
<script src="../core/entities/entity3D_v02.js" defer></script>
<script src="../core/ai/ai_path_v01.js" defer></script>
```

Fig. 4.22. Example of the villagers walking.

ADDING MONSTERS AND MOVING THEM

For now, we've created a peaceful village, but it's time to include monsters in the map. The operation is the same as for the villagers but in this case the intelligence that we'll use will be more unpredictable, as it will be based on chance. You can view and download the final version here:

https://www.thefiveplanets.org/b01/c04/16-map-monsters.html.

The first step is the same as in the previous example, adding the template that will be the basis for cloning the monsters. The template name is *aliendog* and it uses the 3D model *"data/models/monsters/aliendog.dae"*. Note that we've changed the value of the property *"ai"* to *"RandomAI"* in the template. This is how we specify the new class that writes the artificial intelligence.

Now we only need to add the monsters to the map, in this case nine of them. For each one we specify the template and the starting position, but we also add four more properties (*minX, maxX, minZ, maxZ*) to mark the area of the rectangle in which the monster can move about randomly.

```
$RG.templates={

    ...

    "aliendog": {
        "model": "../data/models/monsters/aliendog.dae",
        "type":1, "animation":true,
        "ai":"RandomAI",
        "scale":{"x":0.05,"y":0.05,"z":0.05},
        "rotate":{"x":-90,"y":0,"z":-90}
    }

    ...

$WORLD.map = {
    "map3D": [
        { "template": "aliendog", "x": 70, "z": 120, "minX":60,"maxX":85,"minZ":117,"maxZ":140},
        { "template": "aliendog", "x": 73, "z": 150, "minX":60,"maxX":85,"minZ":140,"maxZ":163},
        { "template": "aliendog", "x": 80, "z": 170, "minX":60,"maxX":85,"minZ":163,"maxZ":186},
        { "template": "aliendog", "x": 65, "z": 190, "minX":60,"maxX":85,"minZ":186,"maxZ":209},
        { "template": "aliendog", "x": 90, "z": 140, "minX":85,"maxX":111,"minZ":117,"maxZ":140},
        { "template": "aliendog", "x": 100, "z": 141, "minX":85,"maxX":111,"minZ":140,"maxZ":163},
        { "template": "aliendog", "x": 95, "z": 149, "minX":85,"maxX":111,"minZ":163,"maxZ":186},
        { "template": "aliendog", "x": 105, "z": 149, "minX":85,"maxX":111,"minZ":186,"maxZ":209},
        { "template": "aliendog", "x": 105, "z": 149, "minX":90,"maxX":110,"minZ":132,"maxZ":150}
    ]
```

```
};
```

Fig. 4.23. Example of monsters walking.

Creating basic Artificial Intelligence through unpredictable movement

Now we just need to write the logic for the artificial intelligence. We've created a new JavaScript file *"core\ai\ai_random_v01.js"*, in which we define the class *$AIS.RandomAI*.

We instantiate the class indicating the *mesh* and the properties of the map element. In this case the algorithm waits to find the properties that mark the area of displacement (*minX, maxX, minZ, maxZ*), and optionally the speed (*velocity*).

In this class, we've defined the function *$AIS.RandomAI.prototype.changeDirection*, which calculates the direction of travel, so that the monster will move in this direction until it reaches the edge of the displacement area. In this case, it will be called again to calculate a new travel direction and to prevent it from leaving the marked area.

The method **update** (*$AIS.RandomAI.prototype.update*) will call from the animation loop, so that the position of the monster will be updated over time. It's at this point when we'll check if it leaves the area of displacement. If it has then we'll calculate a new vector of direction.

The full code of the file *ai_random_v01.js* is as follows:

```
var $AIS = $AIS || {};

$AIS.RandomAI = function (object, prop) {
    this._object=object;
    this.velocity=3; //unidades por segundo
```

```
        if (prop.velocity) {  this.velocity=prop.velocity;  };
        this.minX=prop.minX;
        this.maxX=prop.maxX;
        this.minZ=prop.minZ;
        this.maxZ=prop.maxZ;
        this.directionWalk = new THREE.Vector3(0.5, 0, 0.5);
        this.changeDirection();
};

$AIS.RandomAI.prototype.changeDirection = function () {
        this._lastRandomX = Math.random();
        this._lastRandomZ = 1 - this._lastRandomX;
        if (Math.random() < 0.5) {
            this._lastRandomX = this._lastRandomX * -1;
        }
        if (Math.random() < 0.5) {
            this._lastRandomZ = this._lastRandomZ * -1;
        }
        this.directionWalk.x = this._lastRandomX;
        this.directionWalk.z = this._lastRandomZ;
        var pos = this.directionWalk.clone();
        pos.add(this._object.position);
        this._object.lookAt(pos);
};

$AIS.RandomAI.prototype.update = function ( delta ) {
        var p=this._object.position;
        var x=p.x+ this.directionWalk.x * this.velocity * delta;
        var z=p.z+ this.directionWalk.z * this.velocity * delta;
        var bChange=false;
        if (x<this.minX) {
            x=this.minX;bChange=true;
        } else if (x>this.maxX) {
            x=this.maxX;bChange=true;
        };
        if (z<this.minZ) {
            z=this.minZ;bChange=true;
        } else if (z>this.maxZ) {
            z=this.maxZ;bChange=true;
        };
        if (bChange) {
            this.changeDirection();
        };
        p.set(x, p.y, z)
};
```

```
$AIS.RandomAI.prototype.getPosition = function ( ) {
    return this._object.position;
};
```

C5 - THREEJS: EXPLORING AND INTERACTING

In this chapter, we'll explain how to interact with our scenes and games using the keyboard and mouse. We'll also make our first version of the controller to move our main character manually, thus advancing the development of first person role-playing game.

We'll also learn how to use a webcam in order to detect body movement to interact with our web pages or applications.

FIRST-PERSON BASIC CONTROLLER – MOVEMENT WITH KEYBOARD AND MOUSE

Based on the controller with the camera was moving along a fixed path, we'll modify it so that we can move the camera manually with the keyboard and mouse. We can move forward, backward or sideways by using the arrow keys or the key combination *WASD*. We also can turn the camera if we use the mouse and position the cursor on the left and right-hand side of the screen, and if we are moving we can change the travel direction. By pressing the *SHIFT* key, we can increase the speed, and simulate running.

To begin with, we'll add the instructions to capture events on the keyboard: *keyDown* to detect when we start to press a key and *keyUp* to detect when we finish pressing it.

We've defined the following properties within the controller: *moveFoward*, *moveBackward*, *moveRight*, *moveLeft* and *run*. We change the value of *moveForward* to *true* when we press the "W" key or the forward arrow and we change the value to *false* when we release the key. The same applies to the property *moveBackward*, but with the "S" key or the back arrow. The property *moveRight* will have the value *true* if we press the "A" key or the right arrow. The property "*moveLeft*" is linked with the" D " key or right arrow. Finally, we'll change the property *run* with the *SHIFT* key. Thus, from the animation loop we can update the position of the camera just by checking the value of these four properties.

We've created a new JavaScript file *"core/controls/controls_v01.js"* to implement the controller logic. We've built on the map we created in the previous chapter, which contained monsters and villagers moving through it, as an example, but we've replaced the controller that moved the camera along a predetermined path to the new one. You can see the complete example here:

https://www.thefiveplanets.org/b01/c05/01-controls.html.

The first will record events on the keyboard:

```
var $CONTROLS = $CONTROLS || {};
$CONTROLS.FirstPersonControls = function ( object, domElement ) {
    ...
    this.onKeyDown = function ( event ) {
        switch ( event.keyCode ) {
            case 38: /*up*/
            case 87: /*W*/
                this.moveForward = true;
                break;
            case 37: /*left*/
            case 65: /*A*/
                this.moveLeft = true;
                break;
            case 40: /*down*/
            case 83: /*S*/
                this.moveBackward = true;
                break;
            case 39: /*right*/
            case 68: /*D*/
                this.moveRight = true;
                break;
            case 16: /*shift*/
                this.run = true;
                break;
        }
    };

    this.onKeyUp = function ( event ) {
        switch ( event.keyCode ) {
            case 38: /*up*/
            case 87: /*W*/
                this.moveForward = false;
                break;
            case 37: /*left*/
            case 65: /*A*/
                this.moveLeft = false;
                break;
            case 40: /*down*/
            case 83: /*S*/
                this.moveBackward = false;
                break;
            case 39: /*right*/
            case 68: /*D*/
```

```
                this.moveRight = false;
                break;
            case 16: /*shift*/
                this.run = false; break;
        }
    };
    ...
    var _onKeyDown = bind( this, this.onKeyDown );
    var _onKeyUp = bind( this, this.onKeyUp );
    ...
    window.addEventListener( 'keydown', _onKeyDown, false );
    window.addEventListener( 'keyup', _onKeyUp, false );
    ...
}
```

The JavaScript key that triggers the event is identified by a numerical code accessible from the property *event.keyCode*. For example, the "W" key is associated with the code 87.

Now we must do the same with the mouse. To do this we'll capture the event *mousemove* to detect if the mouse is in the right half or the left half of the screen. We'll save the number of pixels that separate the property *mouseX* from the middle of the screen, and we'll know whether it's on the right or left by looking at the number sign. This allows us to calculate the rotational direction and the speed; the further toward the edges of the screen the faster it is.

```
this.onMouseMove = function ( event ) {
    if ( this.domElement === document ) {
        this.mouseX = event.pageX - this.viewHalfX;
    } else {
        this.mouseX = event.pageX - this.domElement.offsetLeft - this.viewHalfX;
    }
};
```

Now we are ready to create the method *update (delta)* to update the position of the camera. We'll call the function from the animation loop, by giving the time since the last execution as a parameter. *Update* will run sixty times per second in an optimum state. The update function, in this case, is as follows.

```
this.update = function (delta) {
    if ( this.enabled === false ) return;
    var actualMoveSpeed = delta * (this.run?this.movementSpeedRun:this.movementSpeed);
    if ( this.moveForward ) this.object.translateZ( - ( actualMoveSpeed ) );
    if ( this.moveBackward ) this.object.translateZ( actualMoveSpeed );
    if ( this.moveLeft ) this.object.translateX( - actualMoveSpeed );
    if ( this.moveRight ) this.object.translateX( actualMoveSpeed );
```

```
this.object.position.y=this.eyeY;
if (this.minX>this.object.position.x) {
    this.object.position.x=this.minX;
} else if (this.maxX<this.object.position.x) {
    this.object.position.x=this.maxX;
}
if (this.minZ>this.object.position.z) {
    this.object.position.z=this.minZ;
} else if (this.maxZ<this.object.position.z) {
    this.object.position.z=this.maxZ;
}
if (this.showPosition) {
    this.panelInfo.innerHTML=" x: "+Math.round(this.object.position.x,0.1)+" z: "+
    Math.round(this.object.position.z,0.1)+" ";
}
var actualLookSpeed = delta * this.lookSpeed;
this.lon += this.mouseX * actualLookSpeed;
this.theta = THREE.Math.degToRad( this.lon );
var targetPosition = this.target,
position = this.object.position;
targetPosition.x = position.x + 100 * Math.cos( this.theta );
targetPosition.z = position.z + 100 * Math.sin( this.theta );
this.object.lookAt( targetPosition );
};
```

The property *this.object* point it at the camera, which is one of the parameters given to instantiate the class. In the code, we use the *flags (moveFoward, moveBackward, moveRight, moveLeft)* to determine the direction in which we move the camera. For example, the following statement *"if (this.moveLeft) this.object.translateX(- actualMoveSpeed);"* moves the camera to the left.

As a last step, in the main HTML file (*01-controls.html*) we've replaced the controller with the new one:

```
<script src="../core/controls/controls_v01.js" defer></script>
```

We've also replaced the instructions to create the controller. Now we no longer need to specify the path of movement, as we can now move freely.

```
$WORLD.controls = new $CONTROLS.FirstPersonControls ($WORLD.camera);
$WORLD.controls.minX=60;
$WORLD.controls.minZ=117;
$WORLD.controls.maxX=226;
$WORLD.controls.maxZ=209;
$WORLD.controls.showPosition();
$WORLD.addToListUpdate ($WORLD.controls);
```

Note that the controller is included in the update list when running the instruction *$WORLD.addToListUpdate($WORLD.controls)*.

The properties we've added to the controller are the following:

enabled = true	Enable or disable the controller.
movementSpeed = 1.0	Moving speed.
lookSpeed = 0.005	Speed of rotation of the camera.
minX	Minimum position on the x-axis.
maxX	Maximum position on the x-axis.
minZ	Minimum position on the z-axis.
maxZ	Maximum position on the z-axis.

THREE.JS CONTROLLERS

Most applications are controlled in similar ways, depending on the type of application and the device used. *Three.js* provides a native set of controllers that can be used in most situations, which are in the folder "*examples\js\controls*" and must be loaded in order to be used.

In this case, I admit that we've created our first example from the controller *FirstPersonControls.js,* but we've simplified and adapted it to our needs. The original version allows us to turn the camera up and down, in addition to being able to move vertically, which are options that are not of relevance to the game we are developing.

To create our applications and web pages, it's best to copy the controller that best suits our needs and adapt it, instead of writing a new one every time.

Now we can see what *Three.js* offers us by default to move the camera:

FirstPersonControls.js

FirstPersonControls.js offers a first-person view, allowing you to control the camera using the keyboard and mouse. The keys *WASD* or arrows allow us to move forward/left/back/right, we move up with "R" and down with "F" and we use the mouse to look around. This controller is usually used for first-person shooting games.

Parameter	Description
enabled = true	Enable or disable the controller.
movementSpeed = 1.0	Moving speed.
lookSpeed = 0.005	Speed of the rotation of the camera.
lookVertical = true	Enable or disable turning the camera vertically.

activeLook = true	Enable or disable turning of the camera, to simulate turning one's head sideways.
heightSpeed = false	If enabled, the upward movement is simulated as if it were a jump.

You can see a complete example here:

https://www.thefiveplanets.org/b01/c05/02-first-person-controls.html.

FlyControls.js

This simulates levitation. The *WASD* keys allow movement forward/left/back/right, while we move up and down with "R" and "F" keys, and we turn the screen with "Q" and "E". If we move the mouse or the arrows we turn to simulate the movement of the head. With the left mouse button, we go forward and with the right button we go backwards.

Parameter	Description
enabled = true	Enable or disable the controller.
movementSpeed = 1.0;	Speed of movement.
rollSpeed = 0.005	Speed of the rotation of the camera.
dragToLook = false;	When activating this property, we must press the left button of the mouse to turn the camera.

You can see a complete example here:

https://www.thefiveplanets.org/b01/c05/03-fly-controls.html.

OrbitControls.js

This control is especially designed for touch screens. It allows us to control the scene using the mouse or with our fingers on a touch screen. We can rotate the scene by pressing the left mouse button and moving it, or dragging it with a finger. Furthermore, we can enlarge or shrink the scene by pressing the middle mouse button or the *scroll* wheel, or by using two fingers on the screen. Pressing the right mouse button or the arrows, or pressing the touchpad with three fingers, moves the camera up, down, left or right. It's usually used to examine and rotate a single object, allowing it to see from all angles.

Parameter	Description
enableZoom = true;	Activate or deactivate zoom.
zoomSpeed = 1.0;	Zoom speed.
enableRotate = true;	Enable or disable rotation of the scene.
rotateSpeed = 1.0;	Speed of rotation.
autoRotate = false	Enable automatic rotation. In this case, you must make sure to call the function *update* from the animation loop.

autoRotateSpeed = 2.0   The seconds it takes to complete a full round.
enableKeys = true   Enable or disable the keyboard keys.

Click on the following link to see a complete example:

https://www.thefiveplanets.org/b01/c05/04-orbit-controls.html.

TrackballControls.js

This control is a lot like the previous one, but the main difference between the two is that this one does not allow the player to control the camera by using the keyboard, but only by using the mouse or touch screen. So, it's especially useful when there are several CANVASES on one screen. An example of this would be, an online store where each product is displayed in 3D and can rotate individually, without affecting the rest.

You can see a complete example here:

https://www.thefiveplanets.org/b01/c05/05-trackball-controls.html.

CONTROLLING MOVEMENT VIA WEBCAM (WEBRTC)

In this section, we'll learn how to detect user movement through a Webcam. With this technique, we can control our games or web creations through movement, without using a keyboard or joystick. The first example we'll look at shows how to press a series of buttons distributed within the range of vision of the camera, as shown in the figure below.

Fig. 5.02. Example of control via webcam.

As you can see we've added six buttons at the top, which we'll activate by moving our hand or an object over them. The buttons are divided into two blocks, on the right there are three, which when activated cause a message to appear on the screen indicating which of them is active. If it's red, it specifies that we are "running"; if it's yellow that we are "walking" and if it's green we are "standing still". In case we are running or walking, with the three buttons on the right we will control the direction, so that the message will specify if we are moving to the right, left or forward.

We'll use the *API getUserMedia* of *HTML5*, which is part of the *WebRTC* technology, as it allows us to record audio or video using a webcam, as well as edit, and even share the recording with other computers. Because of its power, there are user groups that tell you how to block it to prevent images or our IP being obtained without our consent.

This technology is perfect for creating connections between computers like voice and video *chats*, but that goes beyond the objective of this first book, so we'll deal with it at a later stage.

Click on the following link to access the full sample and download the complete code:

https://www.thefiveplanets.org/b01/c05/06-webcam-motion-detection.html.

We'll create a very simple controller for our game from this primary example, so that we can navigate around the map by moving our hands.

Access to the webcam (HTML5 getUserMedia API)

The first step is to access the webcam. This is very easy with *WebRTC*, currently supported by most modern browsers except Safari. Among the different browsers there are small differences in syntax, so we can download the **adapter.js** library, which solves these problems for us.

https://github.com/webrtc/adapter

The other point to consider is that this technology to run it requires a secure connection *SSL (https)* for security reasons and a message appears requesting the user's permission to access the webcam, which is an extra complication that forces us to manage certificates. Obviously, if we execute the code locally or from a hybrid application, this point can be solved in another way.

To collect the *stream* of the webcam, we create an element *<video>* in HTML code. In this case this element should be hidden to prevent it from being seen.

```
<video id="monitor" autoplay style="display: none; width: 320px; height: 240px;"></video>
```

Now we add a bit of JavaScript, and the video recorded by the webcam will dump into the element **"monitor"**.

```
// Detection of WebRTC availability
if (!navigator.mediaDevices) {
    document.getElementById('messageError').innerHTML =
    'Lo sentimos. La tecnología WebRTC no esta disponible.';
}
```

```
// Capture the video from the WebCam
navigator.mediaDevices.getUserMedia({
        audio: false,
        video: {width: 320, height: 240}
    })
    .then(gotStream)
    .catch(errorStream);

function gotStream(stream) {
    var camvideo = document.getElementById('monitor');
    camvideo.srcObject = stream;
    camvideo.onerror = function(e) {
        stream.stop();
    };
    stream.onended = errorStream;
};

function errorStream(e) {
    var msg = 'No hay camara disponible o el código se ejecuta desde un servidor no seguro.';
    if (e.code == 1) {   msg = 'El usuario ha denegado el acceso a la cámara.';   }
    document.getElementById('errorMessage').textContent = msg;
}
```

Creating the interface

We must record two video images at two different moments to detect movement. We compare these images with each other, so that we know there is movement in areas where they do not coincide. In this case, we'll use the function *requestAnimation*, which will record approximately sixty frames per second.

To record the image, we'll use a HTML canvas element (*id = "videoCanvas"*), which in turn will also show the last image recorded by the camera. We'll paint another HTML canvas element (*id = "buttonsLayer"*) on this layer, which we'll use to display six buttons. Finally, we'll use a third HTML canvas element (*"Id = blendCanvas"*), which shows a picture in black and white, and highlights pixels in white that do not match those in the last two video images recorded. This allows us to know exactly where there is movement. We usually keep this last element hidden (*diplay = "none"*), but for the purposes of demonstration we'll display it.

Thus, the code to create the interface is as follows:

```
<div id="canvasLayers" width="320" height="240" style="position: absolute; right: 0px; top: 0px; width: 320px;
height: 240px; overflow:hidden;">
    <canvas id="videoCanvas" width="320" height="240" style="z-index: 1; position: absolute; left:0px;
top:0px;width: 320px; height: 240px; overflow:hidden;"></canvas>
```

```
        <canvas id="buttonsLayer" width="320" height="240" style="z-index: 2; position: absolute; left:0px; top:0px;
opacity:0.5;width: 320px; height: 240px; overflow:hidden;"></canvas>
    </div>
    <script>

...

var buttonsLayerCanvas = document.getElementById( 'buttonsLayer' );
var buttonsLayerContext = buttonsLayerCanvas.getContext( '2d' );

...

var buttons = [];

var button1 = new Image();
button1.onload=function(){drawButton(0)};
var buttonData1 = { name:"wait", image:button1, x:64 + 10, y:10, w:32, h:32, pressed:false  };
buttons.push( buttonData1 );
button1.src ="../data/graphics/ui/ico/wait-icon.png";

var button2 = new Image();
button2.onload=function(){drawButton(1)};
var buttonData2 = { name:"walking", image:button2, x: 32 + 10, y:10, w:32, h:32, pressed:false };
buttons.push( buttonData2 );
button2.src ="../data/graphics/ui/ico/walking-icon.png";

var button3 = new Image();
button3.onload=function(){drawButton(2)};
var buttonData3 = { name:"runing", image:button3, x:10, y:10, w:32, h:32, pressed:false };
buttons.push( buttonData3 );
button3.src ="../data/graphics/ui/ico/running-icon.png";

...

function drawButton(i){
    buttonsLayerContext.drawImage( buttons[i].image, buttons[i].x, buttons[i].y, buttons[i].w, buttons[i].h );
}

...
```

Note that we create an array with the list of buttons, indicating for each the position where it starts (*x*, *y*), the width (*w*), the height (*h*) and a boolean (*pressed*) that will enable us to always see if the button is being pressed. In this case a button is pressed while we move our finger or another object over it.

Capturing the two images

With the interface created we must capture the two images. We have defined two global variables to do this: ***currentImageData*** to save the last recorded frame and ***lastImageData*** for the penultimate. In both images, we can individually access pixels using the property *data*, which contains an array of integers (0 to 255), so that each set of four integers forms a pixel:

currentImageData.data[0] – Amount of red in the first pixel.
currentImageData.data[1] – Amount of green in the first pixel.
currentImageData.data [2] – Amount of blue in the first pixel.
currentImageData.data[3] – Alpha specifies the transparency of the colour (255 is fully opaque).

The way to transfer the video image HTML element to the canvas element is with *drawImage,* whereas with *getImageData* we record the array of pixels.

```
var monitor = document.getElementById( 'monitor' );
var videoCanvas = document.getElementById( 'videoCanvas' );
var videoContext = videoCanvas.getContext( '2d' );
...
var lastImageData;
var currentImageData;
function getCurrentImageData()
{
    videoContext.drawImage( monitor, 0, 0, videoCanvas.width, videoCanvas.height );
    lastImageData = currentImageData;
    currentImageData = videoContext.getImageData(0, 0, videoCanvas.width, videoCanvas.height);
    if (!lastImageData) lastImageData = currentImageData;
}
...
animate();
...
function animate() {
  requestAnimationFrame( animate );
    if ( monitor.readyState === monitor.HAVE_ENOUGH_DATA )   {
      getCurrentImageData();
        ...
  }
};
```

Comparing the last two frames of the camera

Now that we have the two loaded images, we'll compare them pixel by pixel and create a third image of two colours. The colour white specifies that the pixels are completely different, while the colour black specifies that they are identical or similar.

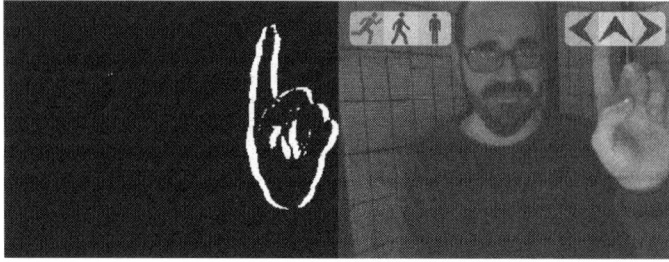

Fig. 5.03. Black and white image showing the moving part.

An easy way to compare the three colours (red, green, blue) of a pixel with those of the other image, is by subtracting their values. If the result is close to 0 for all of the three values (for example a value between -31 and 31) we'll assume that there is no a significant variation, so the pixel of the new image will be black, and will be white in the opposite case. It's advisable to adjust the tolerance value between 31 and 63 depending on the camera. The JavaScript code to build the third image is as follows:

```
var blendedImageData = blendContext.createImageData(videoCanvas.width, videoCanvas.height);
var blendedData= blendedImageData.data;
// Remove transparency
for (var i = 0;i < (blendedData.length);i+=4)
{
    blendedData[i+3] = 0xFF;
}
..
function blend()
{
    differenceAccuracy(blendedData.data, currentImageData.data, lastImageData.data);
    blendContext.putImageData(blendedData, 0, 0);
}


function differenceAccuracy(target, data1, data2) {
    if (data1.length != data2.length) return null;
    for (var i = 0;i < (data1.length);i+=4) {
        var diff=(fastAbs(data1[i] - data2[i]) > 31 || fastAbs(data1[i+1] - data2[i+1]) > 31 ||
fastAbs(data1[i+2] - data2[i+2]) > 31)? 0xFF : 0;
        target[i]   = diff;
        target[i+1] = diff;
        target[i+2] = diff;
    }
};
function fastAbs(value) {
    return (value ^ (value >> 31)) - (value >> 31);
}
```

Determining the buttons or screen areas that show movement

The only thing left to do is to compare if there is movement in the areas enclosed by the buttons. To do this, we'll try each button and if the number of white pixels exceeds 20% we'll consider that the button is pressed, and if not that it's disabled.

```
function checkAreas() {
    for (var b = 0; b < buttons.length; b++) {
        var blendedData = blendContext.getImageData(
            buttons[b].x,
            buttons[b].y,
            buttons[b].w,
            buttons[b].h );

        var sum = 0;
        var countPixels = blendedData.data.length * 0.25;
        for (var i = 0;i < (blendedData.data.length);i+=4) {
            sum += blendedData.data[i];
        }
        var average = Math.round(sum / countPixels);
        if (average > 50) { //20%
            buttons[b].pressed=true;
        } else {
            buttons[b].pressed=false;
        }
    }
};
```

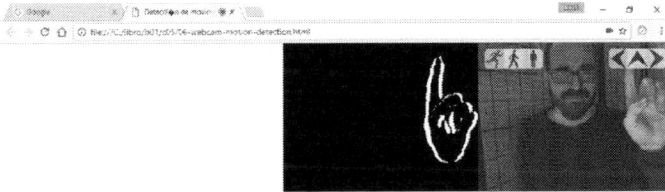

We are walking and we are going forward.

Fig. 5.04. Image of the final example.

Now we are ready to show the action that we are performing according to the buttons that are being pressed on the screen. To do this we'll monitor the state of the buttons in the animation loop, as shown below:

...

```
animate();

var action="standing";
var action2="forward";

function animate() {
    requestAnimationFrame( animate );
    if ( monitor.readyState === monitor.HAVE_ENOUGH_DATA ) {
        getCurrentImageData();
        blend();
        checkAreas();

        if (buttonData3.pressed) {
            action="running";
        } else if (buttonData2.pressed) {
            action="walking";
        } else if (buttonData1.pressed) {
            action="standing";
        };

        if (buttonData5.pressed) {
            action2="adelante";
        } else if (buttonData6.pressed) {
            action2="the right";
        } else if (buttonData4.pressed) {
            action2="the left";
        };

        var msg =" We are " + action;
        if (action!="standing"){
            msg +=" we are going to "+action2;
        };
        messageArea.innerHTML = "<font size='+4'><b>" + msg + ".</b></font>";
    }
}
```

Applying movement control to the game

From the previous example, we have incorporated motion detection to the controller of the main character. Now we can control the character by using the keyboard, mouse, and even the movement of our body. The controller code is *"core\controls\controls_webcam_v01.js"*.

Click on the following link to access the full example and to download the controller code:
https://www.thefiveplanets.org/b01/c05/07-controls-motion-detection.html

Next I will show the photo resulting from the example.

Fig. 5.05. Picture of the game controlled by movement.

CONTROLING WEBPAGES WITH GAMES CONSOLE CONTROL PADS

An important consideration in the creation of a videogame is deciding on the manner in which the game will be controlled. Nowadays with the popularity of game consoles (Xbox, PlayStation, Wii, etc.) many users have grown accustomed to using *gamepads* and *joysticks* for this purpose.

Fig. 5.06. PlayStation controller (Dual Shock 4).

These devices are also available for the PC as an alternative to the mouse and keyboard. Their use on our webpages could help widen our audience to include those who are more used to game consoles. They are also perfect for controlling applications and webpages made for *Smart TVs*.

Fortunately, there is an *API* in *HTML5* with which we can access these devices easily. (https://www.w3.org/TR/gamepad/)

The API is made up of the following elements:

- The incorporation of two new events (***gamepadconnected*** and ***gamepaddisconnected***), to detect the connection and disconnection of a gamepad.
- The ability to recognise multiple gamepads using the ***navigator.getGamepads()*** method to obtain the complete list. In theory, we could have various control pads, each connected to its own *USB port*.
- The ability to inspect each gamepad, identify how many buttons and joysticks it has, and see the status of each of these elements.

API Detection

For the time being, this technology is only compatible with Firefox and Chrome. Both have a *navigator.getGamepads()* method that returns the list of available control pads, so the easiest way to know if a browser supports this API is to verify if the *getGamepads()* method *exists*. This is the simple function code for verifying this:

```
function canGame() {
    return "getGamepads" in navigator;
}
```

Gamepad Events

The webpage will activate the *gamepadconnected* event when a new game controller is connected to the computer. This will only happen when the user either presses a button or moves a joystick. In Firefox, the list of controllers will only be accessible once this event has been launched, which means the user has interacted with the gamepad. Once one of the gamepad has been activated the list will return complete.

When a gamepad is disconnected the *gamepaddisconnected* event will launch.

Unfortunately, events are not available in every web browser, so we must repeatedly call the *getGamepads* method until it returns the list of controllers, and then launch the event manually. We can execute the query second by second with *setInterval*, for example, until it appears.

An initial version, using *JQuery* to enable event capture, would be as follows:

```
var hasGP = false;
function canGame() {
    return "getGamepads" in navigator;
```

```
};

$(document).ready(function() {
  if(canGame()) {

    ...
    $(window).on("gamepadconnected", function() {
      hasGP = true;
      console.log("connection event");

      ...
    });

    $(window).on("gamepaddisconnected", function() {
      console.log("disconnection event");

      ...
    });

    //setup an interval for Chrome
    var checkGP = window.setInterval(function() {
      console.log('checkGP');
      if(navigator.getGamepads()[0]) {
        if(!hasGP) $(window).trigger("gamepadconnected");

        ...
      }
    }, 500);
  }

});
```

Get the list of objects of gamepad type

Now that we have determined if there is at least one gamepad connected, we can monitor the status of the buttons and analogue sticks. We usually execute the query from an animation loop (with *requestAnimationFrame* or *setInterval,* for example*),* from where we update the scene according to the state of the gamepad.

We obtain the list of controllers with *navigator.getGamepads*(), where each entry is an object with the following properties:

- **id**: A string of characters containing the name of the controller. Don't expect friendly descriptions here. In *Firefox*, my controller "*Dual Shock 4*" (*PlayStation*) is called "*54c-5c4-Wireless Controller*", while in *Chrome* the same controller is "*Wireless Controller (STANDARD GAMEPAD Vendor: 054c Product: 05c4*".

- **index**: A unique integer number for each control pad connected to the system (1, 2, 3, etc.).

- **mapping**: A string of characters that indicates whether the browser has identified the controller and can perform default mapping of the buttons and joysticks (see image of a standard controller – *Fig. 05.07*). If the browser is capable of assigning the device's buttons and joysticks, the value of the *mapping* property will be "*standard*".
- **connected**: This is a Boolean that indicates whether the controller is still connected to the system. If connected the value will be *true,* if not *false.*
- **buttons**: An *array* where each entry corresponds to an object *instance* of the *GamepadButton* class. Each entry has two properties: *pressed* and *value*. The first indicates whether the button has been pressed, the second indicates the force with which we are pressing the button (0 represents a button that has not been pressed, and 1 represents a button that has been pressed all the way down).
- **axes**: An *array* that represents the device's joysticks (for example, *analogue thumbsticks*). Given a *gamepad* like the one in the photo (*Fig. 05.06*) with two thumbsticks, we will have an *array* of four elements, where each thumbstick will be represented by 2 values in the *array*. The first of the pair represents the *X axis* (left/right movement), while the second represents the *Y axis* (up/down movement). In all cases the value will oscillate between -1 and 1 (negative values to the left and positive to the right, likewise negative values up and positive down). In accordance with the API's specifications, the *array* is organised according to "importance", so in theory, we can focus on *axes[0]* and *axes[1]* for most gaming needs.

Therefore, according to these indications, with "*gp=navigator.getGamepads()[0]*" we access the first connected controller. With *gp.buttons.length* we know how many buttons it has, and with *gp.axes.length/2* the number of joysticks.

To verify if button two is pressed we only need to check if the "*pressed*" value is *true* (*gp.buttons[2].pressed==true*) and for the left/right axis of the first thumbstick we access *gp.axes[0]*. Here below we see the mapping of the buttons and joysticks for the default controller (*gp.mapping="standar"*).

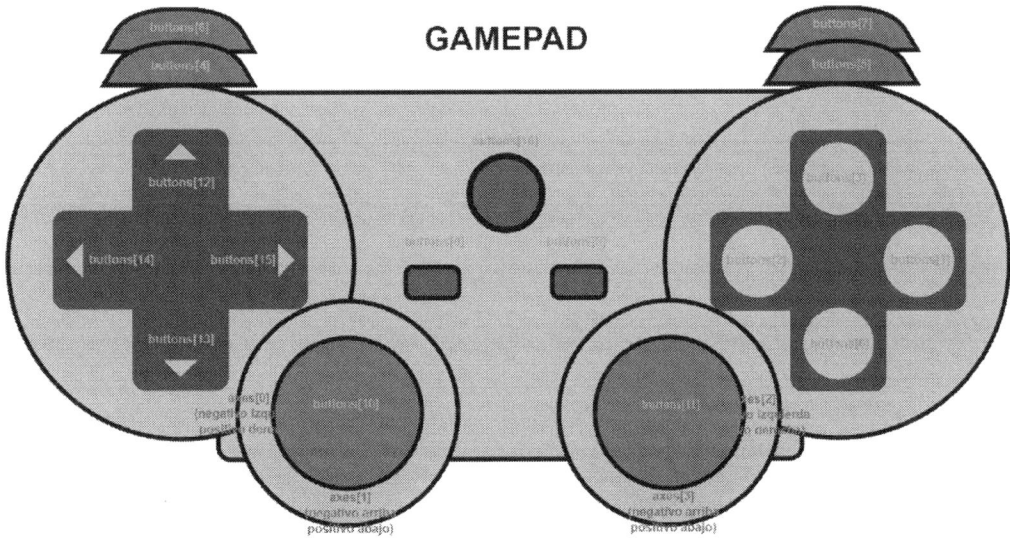

Fig. 5.07. Default button and thumbstick mapping layout.

Unfortunately depending on the device and the manufacturer, we can't always set the device to this layout, and the button configuration can change. Not only that, the performance can change depending on the web browser. In other words, the buttons will change the associated number, and the same goes for joysticks which can be a little chaotic. The solution involves checking if property mapping has the value "*standard*". If it does, then there is no problem because the web browser has identified the controller correctly. If not, we must create an interface that allows us to associate the buttons and each joystick to the action that we want to perform in the game. In any case, if we only use the movement with the values of *axes[0]* and *axes[1]* that is sufficient.

Complete example: viewing gamepad status

In the example, we added a loop with *setInterval* that the first controller obtains, inspects the status of the buttons and joysticks, and displays the values obtained on the screen along with the name of the controller and whether it is configured to the default layout. Here below, the complete code for the example is attached.

```
<!DOCTYPE html>
<html>
<head>
  <meta charset="utf-8">
  <meta http-equiv="X-UA-Compatible" content="IE=edge,chrome=1">
  <meta name="description" content="">
  <meta name="viewport" content="width=device-width">
  <script src="../frameworks/jquery-2.0.3.min.js"></script>
</head>
```

```
<body>
  <div style="text-align: center;">
    <img src="standard_gamepad.svg" style="width:100%;max-width:800px;" />
    <div style="width:100%;max-width:400px;text-align:left;margin: auto;">
      <div id="gamepadPrompt"></div>
      <div id="gamepadDisplay"></div>
    </div>
  </div>
</div>
<script>
var repGP;
var hasGP = false;
function canGame() {
    return "getGamepads" in navigator;
}
$(document).ready(function() {
    if(canGame()) {
        var prompt = " To start using the gamepad, connect it and press any button!";
        $("#gamepadPrompt").text(prompt);
        $(window).on("gamepadconnected", function(e) {
            hasGP = true;
            console.log("connection event");
            $("#gamepadPrompt").html("Gamepad connected!");
            startReportOnGamepad();
        });
        $(window).on("gamepaddisconnected", function(e) {
            console.log("disconnection event");
            $("#gamepadPrompt").text(prompt);
            endReportOnGamepad()
        });
        var checkGP = window.setInterval(function() {
            console.log('checkGP');
            if(navigator.getGamepads()[0]) {
                if(!hasGP) {
                    $(window).trigger("gamepadconnected",{gamepad:navigator.getGamepads()[0]});
                }
                window.clearInterval(checkGP);
            }
        }, 500);
    }
});
function startReportOnGamepad(){
    repGP = window.setInterval(reportOnGamepad,100);
};
function endReportOnGamepad() {
    window.clearInterval(repGP);
};
```

```
function reportOnGamepad() {
    var gp = navigator.getGamepads()[0];
    var html = "";
        html += "<b>id:</b> "+gp.id+"<br/>";
        html += "<b>mapping:<b> "+gp.mapping+"<br/>";
        for(var i=0;i<gp.buttons.length;i++) {
            html+= "<b>buttons[ "+(i)+"]:</b> ";
            if(gp.buttons[i].pressed) html+= " pulsado";
            html+= "<br/>";
        }

        for(var i=0;i<gp.axes.length; i++) {
            html+= "<b>axes["+i+"]:</b> "+gp.axes[i]+"<br/>";
        }

        $("#gamepadDisplay").html(html);
    }
    </script>
    </body>
</html>
```

You can test or download the demo, in either Chrome or Firefox, at the following link: https://www.thefiveplanets.org/b01/c05/08-gamepad.html.

In the following image, we see the screenshot taken when executing the example with a *Dual Shock 4* controller. As you can see, button 6 was being pressed and the left thumbstick pushed up when I took the screenshot.

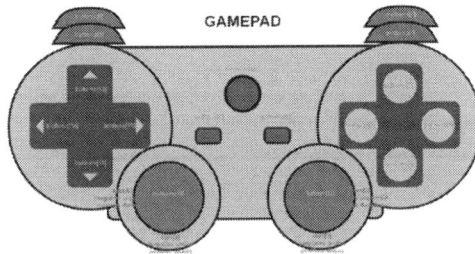

Fig. 5.08. Example using Dual Shock 4 controller.

The values of the axes, when not pressed, usually oscillate between *-0.03* and *0.03*, probably caused by pressure within the controller itself, so it is advisable to set a numerical point from which to exclude values (for example, we will ignore the interval -0.3 to 0.3).

Putting it all together

Now that we have learned the theory, we can perform a more complex example. Starting with the example we opened the chapter with, we have modified it to allow the gamepad to move the camera, as well as doing this with the keyboard and the mouse. In the following link you can see the example in action and download the code: https://www.thefiveplanets.org/b01/c05/09-controls-gamepad.html.

With the left thumbstick we can move forwards, backwards, right and left, while with the right thumbstick we can turn the camera to the sides. Pushing button 4 at the same time we move will make us accelerate, simulating the act of running. The controller code is in *"core\controls\controls_gamepad_v01.js"*. In it we have basically introduced the following changes:

```
$CONTROLS.FirstPersonControls = function ( object, domElement ) {
    ...
    this.hasAPIGamepad= ("getGamepads" in navigator);
    this.haveEventsGamepad = ('ongamepadconnected' in window);
    this.gamepad=null;
    this.update = function( delta ) {
        ...
        if (this.hasAPIGamepad) {
            this.gamepad=navigator.getGamepads()[0];
            if (this.gamepad!=null) {
                bMoveRight=bMoveRight || (this.gamepad.axes[0]>0.3);
                bMoveLeft=bMoveLeft || (this.gamepad.axes[0]<-0.3);
                bMoveBackward=bMoveBackward || (this.gamepad.axes[1]>0.3);
                bMoveForward=bMoveForward || (this.gamepad.axes[1]<-0.3);
                if (this.gamepad.axes.length>2){
                    nRotate=this.gamepad.axes[2]*1500 * actualLookSpeed;
                }
                bRun = bRun || this.gamepad.buttons[4].pressed;
            }
        }
    }
    ...
```

You will notice we have not used the *gamepad* events, but in the *update* function we try to access the first connected controller. If we find one that is connected, we modify the values of the variables that indicate whether we should move, turn or run, according to the gamepad state. Remember that we ignore values between *0.3* and *-0.3* for the axes since the pressure placed on the joysticks is minimal.

SELECTING AND CLICKING ON OBJECTS - RAYCASTER

In this section, we will learn how to select and click on objects using the mouse or the finger on a touchscreen. For this, we will use an example with a scene full of grey cubes. When moving the mouse over the screen, the cube below the arrow will light up red; if there are more than one, it will only select the one closest to the screen. If you press the left mouse button on the selected cube it will change to a greenish-blue colour.

You can see the example in action and download the code at the following link: https://www.thefiveplanets.org/b01/c05/10-raycaster-select-click.html.

Fig. 5.09. Object selection example. The red cube is under the cursor.

How does it work?

At first, this topic can seem easy, but it isn't. Rendering a 3D scene on a 2D screen requires complex calculations, determining where to place each point floating in space on the screen and how the objects are formed according to the camera's angle of focus. This process, converting 3D entities into 2D, is called ***projection***.

But in this case, we want to do exactly the opposite, we want to find out what object is under the mouse pointer, and for this we need to bring those 2D coordinates into the 3D world before trying to see if there is anything behind it. In other words, ***deprojection***.

Once we have the mouse's 3D coordinate, we trace an imaginary line from the camera to our mouse's position, and, following the line, we see which objects we go through, in other words we create rays (***raycaster***). If we poke an object, we will have found what we were looking for. If there are several objects we need only consider the first one we find.

I know this can seem confusing, so let's look at this illustration:

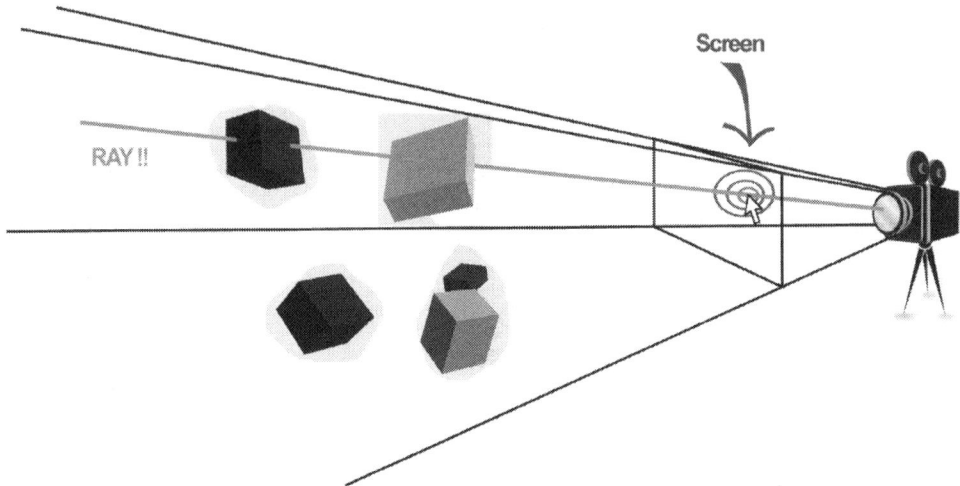

Fig. 5.10. Imaginary line traced from the camera to the mouse's position.

Fortunately, this is very easy to apply with *Three.js*. The library offers the **THREE.raycaster** class that allows us to draw a straight line and, given a list of objects, calculate the points where the ray intersects.

Preparing the scene

But first we are going to start with the basics, create the scene, and add the camera, the lights and the cubes. Specifically, we will add a thousand cubes with the same geometry, but each with its own material, since they have to be different in order to be able to colour them with different shades of grey.

```
<!DOCTYPE html>
<html lang="es">
<head>
    <script src="../frameworks/three.js"></script>
    <script src="../frameworks/stats.js"></script>
</head>
<body>
<script>
    var container, stats;
    var camera, scene, raycaster, renderer;
    var mouse = new THREE.Vector2();
    var SELECTED=null;
    var radius = 100, theta = 0;
    init();
    animate();
    function init() {
        container = document.createElement( 'div' );
        document.body.appendChild( container );
```

```
camera = new THREE.PerspectiveCamera( 70, window.innerWidth / window.innerHeight, 1, 10000 );
scene = new THREE.Scene();
var light = new THREE.DirectionalLight( 0xffffff, 1 );
light.position.set( 1, 1, 1 ).normalize();
scene.add( light );

var geometry = new THREE.BoxBufferGeometry( 20, 20, 20 );
for ( var i = 0; i < 1000; i ++ ) {
    var grey=Math.random();
    var object = new THREE.Mesh( geometry,
    new THREE.MeshLambertMaterial( { color: new THREE.Color( grey, grey , grey ) } ) );
    object.position.x = Math.random() * 800 - 400;
    object.position.y = Math.random() * 800 - 400;
    object.position.z = Math.random() * 800 - 400;
    object.rotation.x = Math.random() * 2 * Math.PI;
    object.rotation.y = Math.random() * 2 * Math.PI;
    object.rotation.z = Math.random() * 2 * Math.PI;
    object.scale.x = Math.random() + 0.5;
    object.scale.y = Math.random() + 0.5;
    object.scale.z = Math.random() + 0.5;
    scene.add( object );
}
renderer = new THREE.WebGLRenderer();
renderer.setClearColor( 0xf0f0f0 );
renderer.setPixelRatio( window.devicePixelRatio );
renderer.setSize( window.innerWidth, window.innerHeight );
renderer.sortObjects = false;
container.appendChild(renderer.domElement);
stats = new Stats();
container.appendChild( stats.dom );
raycaster = new THREE.Raycaster();
document.addEventListener( 'mousemove', onDocumentMouseMove, false );
container.addEventListener( 'mousedown', onDocumentMouseDown, false );
window.addEventListener( 'resize', onWindowResize, false );
}
function onWindowResize() {
    camera.aspect = window.innerWidth / window.innerHeight;
    camera.updateProjectionMatrix();
    renderer.setSize( window.innerWidth, window.innerHeight );
}
function animate() {
    requestAnimationFrame( animate );
    render();
    stats.update();
}
...
```

We have created three variables in the code, which will be the key for the projection:

- *"SELECTED":* Point to the selected cube, in case there isn't a marked cube, its value will be null.
- *"mouse":* Keep the position of the mouse on a 2D vector.
- *"raycaster":* Point to an instance of the **THREE.raycaster** class to create the ray from the camera passing through the mouse's position and calculate the intersections.

Given that we want to select objects when the mouse moves or when we click on them, we have also included the code to capture the events **mousemove** and **mousedown**.

Projecting the line

Now we are prepared to create the ray. With the **THREE.raycaster** class there are two ways that can be used for this:

- *.set (origin, direction):* Sets the ray from the origin position, with the indicated direction.
- *.setFromCamera (2D coordinates, camera):* Given the 2D coordinates of the mouse and the camera, it sets the ray from the camera, crossing through the indicated point.

Furthermore, by indicating the properties **"near"** and **"far"** we can indicate the length of the ray, so that the objects that are out of the indicated range will be ignored. These properties are very useful in first person videogames, for example, in which we only interact with objects that are within reach.

In our case, the method that we are interested in for creating the ray is *setFromCamera,* for which we need to provide the mouse coordinates, but in a normalised format, meaning that for both the X and Y axes the value must be between -1 and 1. With the *mousemove* mouse event we capture its position and perform the calculation of the normalised coordinates:

```
function onDocumentMouseMove( event ) {
    event.preventDefault();
    mouse.x = ( event.clientX / window.innerWidth ) * 2 - 1;
    mouse.y = - ( event.clientY / window.innerHeight ) * 2 + 1;
}
```

The command to create the ray is:

```
raycaster.setFromCamera( mouse, camera );
```

Calculating intersections and selecting the object

In order to find the intersections of the ray we must indicate the list of objects to be verified; in our case, we are going to check with all the objects in the scene, for which the command is as follows:

```
var intersects = raycaster.intersectObjects( scene.children );
```

This will return a list with every intersection of the ray with the cubes, ordered by distance (the closest is first). Each intersection is an object with the following key properties:

- **distance:** Distance between the origin of the ray and the intersection.
- **point:** The exact point where the object is pierced by the ray.
- **object:** The object being pierced.

Consequently, if the list of intersections is not empty (*intersects.length>0*) we know that there is at least one cube under the mouse position. In the *SELECTED* variable we save the last selected cube, so if it is different, we are going to change the colour of the cube to red (*SELECTED.material.emissive.setHex(0xff0000)*) and the form of the mouse pointer to a hand (*container.style.cursor = 'pointer'*).

Before changing the colour of the cube, we save its value in an invented property (*currentHex*); this way we can restore its original colour whenever we lose focus or select another cube.

In this way, the final code is as follows:

```
function render() {
    // find intersections
    raycaster.setFromCamera( mouse, camera );
    var intersects = raycaster.intersectObjects( scene.children );
    if ( intersects.length > 0 ) {
        if ( SELECTED != intersects[ 0 ].object ) {
            if ( SELECTED ) SELECTED.material.emissive.setHex( SELECTED.currentHex );
            SELECTED = intersects[ 0 ].object;
            SELECTED.currentHex = SELECTED.material.emissive.getHex();
            SELECTED.material.emissive.setHex( 0xff0000 );
            container.style.cursor = 'pointer';
        }
    } else {
        if ( SELECTED ) {
            SELECTED.material.emissive.setHex( SELECTED.currentHex );
            SELECTED = null;
            container.style.cursor = 'auto';
        }
    }
}
```

```
      renderer.render( scene, camera );
}
```

Clicking on the object

All that is left now is to program the action to be carried out when we click on the selected cube. For this, in the function invoked by the *mousedown* event, we are going to change the colour of the selected cube to a greenish-blue colour.

```
function onDocumentMouseDown( event ) {
    event.preventDefault();
    if ( SELECTED ){
        SELECTED.currentHex = 0x00ff00*Math.random();
        SELECTED.material.emissive.setHex( SELECTED.currentHex );
    }
}
```

DRAG AND DROP - RAYCASTER

Now we are going to go a little further. Not only will we select objects, we will also move them around the screen. Continuing from the previous example, we have changed the mode so that now instead of randomly adding cubes we have incorporated various utensils that are typical to role-playing games, such as potions, axes, staffs, daggers, piles of coins and a chest. We can freely move all of the objects to any position on the screen, or drag and drop them into the chest.

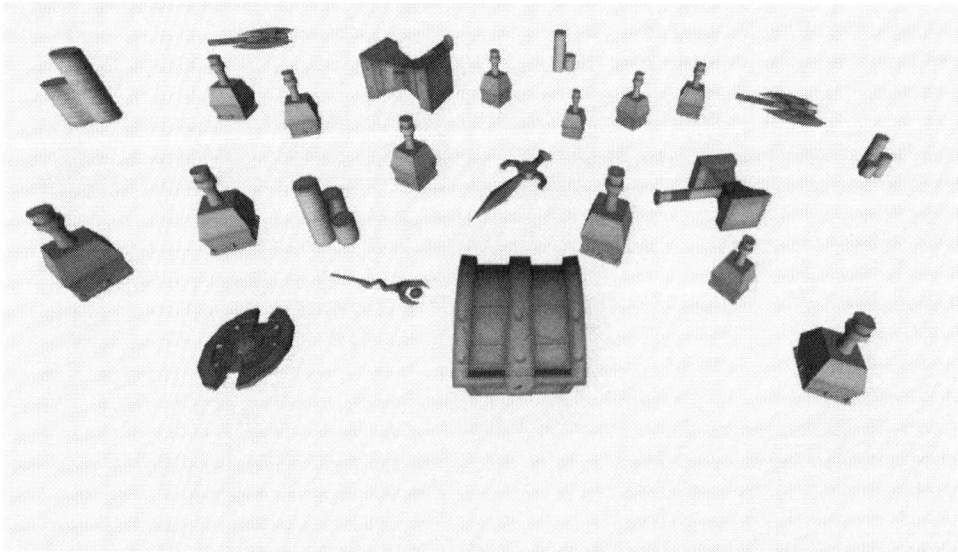

Fig. 5.11. Result of performing the drag and drop example.

So now we are going to have to control the *mouseup* and *mousedown* events, so that, if there is an object under the mouse pointer, with *mousedown* we will initiate the drag action, and with *mousedown* the drop action, while with *mousemove* and the mouse button pressed we will update the object's position so that it moves at the same time as the mouse pointer.

Calculating the position that the 3D object should move to according to the mouse coordinates is not as trivial as it might seem; we must resort to the *THREE.raycaster* object and to an invisible plane. First of all, we will situate the invisible plane parallel to the screen, with the centre in the object's starting position. Secondly, we will create a ray that will go from the camara and pass through the mouse position. The object's new position will be where the ray and the plane intersect. I know that this can seem a little confusing, but the following image makes the concept easier to understand.

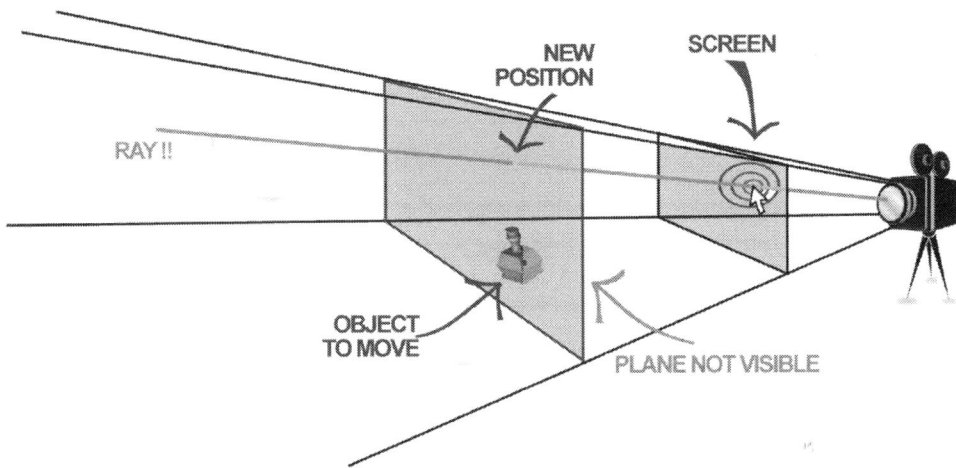

Fig. 5.12. Ray and plane for calculating the object's new position.

In the following link, you can see the example in action and download the code: https://www.thefiveplanets.org/b01/c05/11-raycaster-drag-drop.html.

Preparing the scene

As a first step, we are going to prepare the scene, starting by loading the models of the potions, staffs and weapons that are in *.obj* (*Wavefront*) format. For this, we must include the libraries that are necessary for loading them. Then, we clone the read objects and spread them around the scene. Due to the fact that the code is a little long, I have cut out the repetitive parts, which are easily replicible.

```
<!DOCTYPE html>
<html lang="en">
<head>
  <title>three.js webgl - draggable objects</title>
  <script src="../frameworks/three.js"></script>
```

```
    <script src="../frameworks/stats.js"></script>
    <script src="../frameworks/loaders/MTLLoader.js"></script>
    <script src="../frameworks/loaders/OBJLoader.js"></script>
    <script src="../frameworks/controls/TrackballControls.js"></script>
</head>
<body>
    <script>
    var container, stats;
    var camera, controls, scene, renderer;
    var objects = [];
    var plane = new THREE.Plane();
    var raycaster = new THREE.Raycaster();
    var mouse = new THREE.Vector2();
    var offset = new THREE.Vector3();
    var intersection = new THREE.Vector3();
    var SELECTED, DRAGGED, CHEST;

    init();

    function init() {

        container = document.createElement( 'div' );
        document.body.appendChild( container );

        camera = new THREE.PerspectiveCamera( 70, window.innerWidth / window.innerHeight, 1, 10000 );
        camera.position.z = 6;
        camera.position.y = 5;

        controls = new THREE.TrackballControls( camera );
        ...
        scene = new THREE.Scene();
        ...
        renderer = new THREE.WebGLRenderer( { antialias: true } );
        ...
        container.appendChild( renderer.domElement );

        stats = new Stats();
        container.appendChild( stats.dom );

        renderer.domElement.addEventListener( 'mousemove', onDocumentMouseMove, false );
        renderer.domElement.addEventListener( 'mousedown', onDocumentMouseDown, false );
        renderer.domElement.addEventListener( 'mouseup', onDocumentMouseUp, false );

        window.addEventListener( 'resize', onWindowResize, false );
        loadOBJ ("../data/models/objects/", "potion.mtl", "potion.obj",  scene, function (potion){
        loadOBJ ("../data/models/objects/", "potion2.mtl", "potion.obj",  scene, function (potion2){
```

```
loadOBJ ("../data/models/objects/", "potion3.mtl", "potion.obj", scene, function (potion3){
loadOBJ ("../data/models/objects/", "money.mtl", "money.obj", scene, function (money){
loadOBJ ("../data/models/objects/", "axe.mtl", "axe.obj", scene, function (axe){
loadOBJ ("../data/models/objects/", "hammer.mtl", "hammer.obj", scene, function (hammer){
loadOBJ ("../data/models/objects/", "shield.mtl", "shield.obj", scene, function (shield){
loadOBJ ("../data/models/objects/", "sword.mtl", "sword.obj", scene, function (sword){
loadOBJ ("../data/models/objects/", "staff.mtl", "staff.obj", scene, function (staff){
loadOBJ ("../data/models/objects/", "chest.mtl", "chest.obj", scene, function (chest){
    var object = shield.clone();
    object.position.x = Math.random() * 20 - 10;
    object.position.z = Math.random() * 10 - 10;
    object.rotation.z = Math.PI/2;
    object.rotation.y = Math.random() * 2 * Math.PI;
    scene.add( object );
    objects.push( object );
    object = staff.clone();
    object.position.x = Math.random() * 20 - 10;
    object.position.z = Math.random() * 10 - 10;
    object.rotation.z = Math.PI/2;
    object.rotation.y = Math.random() * 2 * Math.PI;
    scene.add( object );

    ...

    CHEST=chest;
    chest.name="chest";
    object = chest;
    object.position.x = 0;
    object.position.z = 0;
    object.rotation.y = -Math.PI/2;
    scene.add( object );
    objects.push( object );

    animate();

});});});});});});});});});});
}

function onWindowResize() {
    camera.aspect = window.innerWidth / window.innerHeight;
    camera.updateProjectionMatrix();
    renderer.setSize( window.innerWidth, window.innerHeight );
}

function animate() {
    requestAnimationFrame( animate );
    render();
```

```
      stats.update();
  }

  function render() {
    controls.update();
    renderer.render( scene, camera );
  }

  function loadOBJ (path, fileMaterial, fileOBJ, scene, fSuc, fFail) {
    var mtlLoader = new THREE.MTLLoader();
    mtlLoader.setPath(path);
    mtlLoader.load(fileMaterial, function (materials) {
      materials.preload();
      var objLoader = new THREE.OBJLoader();
      objLoader.setMaterials(materials);
      objLoader.setPath(path);
      objLoader.load(fileOBJ, function (object) {
        var mesh=object;
        object.traverse(function (child) {
          if (child instanceof THREE.Mesh) {
            mesh=child;
          }
        });
        fSuc(mesh);
      });
    });
  };
  ...
```

A point worth pointing out is that the objects we will be creating will not only be added to the scene, but also incorporated into an *array* ("*objects*"). We will use this array to detect what objects are found under the mouse pointer; in this way, we will only calculate the intersection of the ray according to the list of objects that can be dragged, instead of comparing them with every object in the scene.

Controlling mouse events

Regarding the previous example, we have created "*DRAGGED*", a new variable that will point to the object that we are dragging with the mouse. We have also created the variable "*offset*", to save the separation between the object's position and the position of the ray's intersection at the moment the mouse button begins to be pressed. In this way, the object's position will be the point of intersection minus the offset (*DRAGGED.position.copy(intersection.sub(offset)*). As in the previous example, the "*SELECTED*" variable saves a pointer at the object found under the mouse.

In this way, the three functions for managing the events are as follows:

```
function onDocumentMouseDown( event ) {
    event.preventDefault();
    if (SELECTED) {
        controls.enabled = false;
        DRAGGED = SELECTED;
        if ( raycaster.ray.intersectPlane( plane, intersection ) ) {
            offset.copy( intersection ).sub( DRAGGED.position );
        }
        container.style.cursor = 'move';
    }
}


function onDocumentMouseMove( event ) {
    event.preventDefault();
    mouse.x = ( event.clientX / window.innerWidth ) * 2 - 1;
    mouse.y = - ( event.clientY / window.innerHeight ) * 2 + 1;

    raycaster.setFromCamera( mouse, camera );

    // Movement of the selected object
    if ( DRAGGED ) {
        if ( raycaster.ray.intersectPlane( plane, intersection ) ) {
            DRAGGED.position.copy( intersection.sub( offset ) );
        }
        return;
    }

    // Selecting the object under the mouse
    var intersects = raycaster.intersectObjects( objects );
    if ( intersects.length > 0 ) {
        if ( SELECTED != intersects[ 0 ].object ) {
            SELECTED = intersects[ 0 ].object;
            plane.setFromNormalAndCoplanarPoint(
                camera.getWorldDirection( plane.normal ),
                SELECTED.position );
        }
        container.style.cursor = 'pointer';
    } else {
        SELECTED = null;
        container.style.cursor = 'auto';
    }
}

function onDocumentMouseUp( event ) {
    event.preventDefault();
```

```
    controls.enabled = true;
    if ( DRAGGED ) {
      if (DRAGGED.name!="chest") {
        var intersects = raycaster.intersectObject( CHEST );
        if ( intersects.length > 0 ) {
          scene.remove(DRAGGED)
        }
      }
      DRAGGED = null;
    }
    container.style.cursor = 'auto';
}
```

You will note that in the ***mousemove*** event, selecting the object with the mouse works practically the same as in the previous example, except that we have added the *"plane.setFromNormalAndCoplanarPoint"* instruction. With this instruction, we move the invisible plane to the object's position and parallel to the screen.

In the ***mousedown*** event, if there is a selected object, we deactivate the keyboard controls and initiate a drag and drop operation, calculating the vector of separation between the object's position and the point of intersection.

Now with the drag and drop operation initiated, we only have to calculate the intersection of the ray with the parallel plane in the *mousemove* event and move the object to this position (**"DRAGGED.position.copy(intersection.sub(offset));"**).

Finally, in the ***mouseup*** event, we verify if the chest is under the mouse pointer. If it is, we eliminate the object we were moving to simulate that we have put it inside the chest.

INTERACTING WITH THE GAME ELEMENTS

Now it's time to see a previous example applied in a real life situation. For this, drawing from the last version of the game, we have modified it to add chests, potions and piles of money in the game map that we can interact with. By clicking on any of these elements a dialogue box will appear similar to the one in the following image.

Fig. 5.13. Dialog box displayed when interacting with the chest.

You can see an example in action and download the code at the following link: https://www.thefiveplanets.org/b01/c05/12-game-pick.html.

In the file *12-game-pick.html* we have introduced the following changes regarding the latest version of the game:

```html
<!DOCTYPE html>
<html lang="es">
<head>

....
<!-- GAME FILES-->
<script src="../core/ui/ui_v02.js" defer></script>
<script src="../core/controls/controls_v02.js" defer></script>
...
<script src="../core/api/api_v01.js" defer></script>
...
<script>
    $RG.templates={
        "chest": {"model": "../data/models/objects/chest.obj",
        "scale":{"x":0.65,"y":0.65,"z":0.65}},
        "money": {"model": "../data/models/objects/money.obj",
        "scale":{"x":0.5,"y":0.5,"z":0.5}},
        "potion": {"model": "../data/models/objects/potion.obj",
        "scale":{"x":0.5,"y":0.5,"z":0.5}},
    }
    $WORLD.map = {
    "map3D": [
        { "template": "chest", "x": 140, "y":0.65, "z": 160, "rY": 75,
        "interact":"$RG.say('El baúl está vacio!')" },
        { "template": "chest", "x": 132, "y":0.65, "z": 137, "rY": -75,
```

```
            "interact":"$RG.say('El baúl está vacío!')" },
         { "template": "money", "x": 152, "y":0.18, "z": 141,
            "interact":"$RG.say('He encontrado un montón de monedas!')" },
            { "template": "potion", "x": 155, "y":0.25, "z": 167,
            "interact":"$RG.say('He encontrado una poción')" }
      ]
      ...
      }
      $UI.draw();

      ...
      $WORLD.controls = new $CONTROLS.FirstPersonControls
         ($WORLD.camera, document, "../data/graphics/ui/ico/spyhole.png");
      $WORLD.controls.verticalMin = -30;
      $WORLD.controls.verticalMax = +30;

      ""
</script>
</head>
```

Note that we have added some additional templates (*chest, money, and potion*).
Furthermore, in the game's map elements, we have incorporated the *"interact"*
property. This property contains JavaScript instructions that indicate the action that
will be performed when we click on an object. For example, clicking on the chest
will execute the "*$RG.say('The chest is empty!')*" instruction shown in the dialogue
box. We have also made other changes but they are not relevant to the subject at
hand and you can try to discover them for yourself.

We have created a new JavaScript file, *"api_v01.js"* where the game's high-level
calls can be added, for example, in this case, the function to show an active message
on screen.

```
$RG.say = function (msg,ch) {
   $UI.timewindow.show(msg,ch);
}
```

The code for creating the dialogue box is in the *"ui.js"* file, along with the logic for
displaying the box and hiding it automatically after 3 seconds. In this case, we have
created a layer that is shown on the canvas, using HTML elements. Another way of
creating the interface is to generate it directly on the *canvas*.

```
//MESSAGE FRAME
$UI.Timewindow = function (cId, oPar) {
   this.id = cId;
   var cVal = '';
   cVal = '<div class="portrait"></div><div class="text_time_window"></div>';

   $('body').append('<div id="' + cId + '" class="ui_time_window" style="display:none">' + cVal + '</div>')
```

```
};
$UI.Timewindow.prototype.show = function (msg,ch) {
    var id = '#' + this.id;
        if (!ch) {
                    ch={"img_face_big":"data/graphics/portraits/mr_who.png"};
        }
    $('#' + this.id).css('display', 'block').find('.portrait').css('background', "url('" +$RG.baseDirectory +
ch.img_face_big + "') no-repeat").css('background-size','100%');
    $('#' + this.id).find('.text_time_window').text(msg);
    try { clearTimeout(this.time_win); } catch (e) { };
    this.time_win=setTimeout(function () { $(id).css('display', 'none'); }, 3000);
};

$UI.Timewindow.prototype.hide = function () {
    $('#' + this.id).css('display', 'none');
};

//DRAW
$UI.draw = function () {
    $UI.timewindow = new $UI.Timewindow("lyr_timewindow");
}
```

The other modified file is "*entity3D_v03.js*". In the function that adds elements to the map, in case it has the *interact* property defined, we will add it to an array (*$WORLD.entitiesInteract*). When we click with the mouse, we will use this array to obtain the object that is found under the mouse pointer and launch the code of the *interact* property.

```
$RG.Entity3D.prototype.addToWorld = function () {

    ...
    //Añadir logica objetos con interacción
    if ("interact" in this.prop) {
        mesh.traverse(function (child) {
            if (child instanceof THREE.Mesh) {
                child.entity3D=self;
                $WORLD.entitiesInteract.push(child);
            }
        });
    };
    ...
}
```

Finally, we have modified the "*controls_v02.js*" file to control the camera turn with the keyboard and not with the mouse, to make interacting with objects using the mouse easier. For this the relevant keys are: *A* or *left arrow* and *D* or *right arrow* to turn the camera horizontally, and the *Start* and *End* keys to turn the camera vertically; while using *Q* and *E* we can move left and right respectively.

We have also added the event *mousedown* that verifies if there is an object under the cursor with which to interact when the mouse button is pressed. If so, we carry out the instructions indicated in the *interact* property. We can perform the same operation by pressing the *I* key, but launching the camera's ray to the centre of the screen. At the same time, we maintain compatibility by controlling the camera with a gamepad, and we assign the action of interacting to button number 5.

```
$CONTROLS.FirstPersonControls = function ( object, domElement ) {
    ...
    this.mouse = new THREE.Vector2();
    this.raycaster = new THREE.Raycaster();
    this.raycaster.far=5;

    ....
    this.onMouseDown= function ( event ) {
        this.interact(this.mouse,this.object);
    };
    this.interact = function(oPointer,oCamara) {
        this.raycaster.setFromCamera( oPointer, oCamara );
        var intersects = this.raycaster.intersectObjects( $WORLD.entitiesInteract);
        if ( intersects.length > 0 ) {
            var mesh=intersects[ 0 ].object;
            if ("entity3D" in mesh && "interact" in mesh.entity3D.prop) {
                eval(mesh.entity3D.prop.interact);
            }
        }
    };
    ...
    this.onMouseMove = function ( event ) {
        this.mouseMovementX = this.mouseMovementX + (event.movementX || 0);
        this.mouseMovementY = this.mouseMovementY + (event.movementY || 0);
        this.mouse.x = ( event.clientX / window.innerWidth ) * 2 - 1;
        this.mouse.y = - ( event.clientY / window.innerHeight ) * 2 + 1;
    };
    ...
    this.onKeyDown = function ( event ) {
        switch ( event.keyCode ) {
            case 73: /*I*/
                this.interact(this.spyhole,this.object);
                break;
```

The example exhibits a significant lack of optimization. At present, we are evaluating the ray with respect to the list of real objects, meaning all the surfaces and vertexes that they are made up of. This implies that the level of calculations is very high, which could have a significant impact on performance. In these cases, it is normal to carry out verifications on more simple shapes, for example, on a cube that encompasses the object. This is the technique that we will use to detect collisions and apply physical laws, so that we are going to have two parallel worlds: one for the graphic representation, and another simpler world made of cubes, spheres and cones in which we will calculate the intersections, collisions and physical laws.

FULL SCREEN (HTML5 FULLSCREEN API)

The emergence of HTML5 has added a large quantity of features. An especially interesting one is the API to display any element in full screen mode. Instead of pressing F11 to make the page take up the entire screen, with this API not only can you show the entire screen but also a single element, image, video or the content of an iframe. On entering full screen mode, a message appears informing the user that they can press ESC at any time to return to standard mode.

Its usefulness is obvious when playing games, using multimedia applications or watching videos, hiding the browser interface and making a better experience possible.

The full screen API is compatible with all the web browsers, including some versions of *Internet Explorer*. Unfortunately, there are still subtle differences and inconsistencies among the browsers and the need to use the manufacturers' prefixes.

Methods, properties and Fullscreen API events

Now I will list the most relevant properties and methods, and how to use them.

- ***document.fullscreenEnabled***

The value of this property is *true* if it is possible to activate full screen mode. On certain occasions, it is not possible to use it, for example, when the document is inside an *<iframe>* element that does not contain the *"allowfullscreen"* attribute. It can also be used to determine if the browser supports the API.

- ***element.requestFullscreen()***

This method allows one single element to be viewed in full screen mode. This function will not always be performed successfully, due to security reasons; it is only available in events the user interacts with: for example, when clicking on an image or a link. Therefore, it cannot be run from events such as *onload*.

To view the entire page in full screen mode the command is as follows:

```
document.documentElement.requestFullscreen()
```

For one single element, an image for example:

```
document.getElementById("my_image").requestFullscreen()
```

This will make the image with the *ID 'my_image'* be shown in full screen mode.

- ***document.exitFullscreen()***

This method cancels full screen mode and returns to the browser's default view.

- ***document.fullscreenElement***

Returns the element that is currently in full screen mode. For example, if it is the entire page, it returns the document itself.

The API offers the following events:

- ***fullscreenchange***

The event is triggered whenever full screen mode is activated or deactivated. The event does not tell you what the final mode is, but you can determine by verifying if the property *document.fullscreenElement* is equal to null.

- ***fullscreenerror***

This activates when it is not possible to open the element in full screen mode, primarily if you try activating the function from an invalid event, or even if the page is inside an *iframe* and you have not been explicitly informed that this action is allowed.

These are the standard methods, but for the moment we still need to use the manufacturer prefixes and even make some name corrections. This is why we will now look at how to implement the *API* in real life.

In the following link, you can see a working example and download the code: https://www.thefiveplanets.org/b01/c05/13-full-screen.html.

Availability detection of the full screen API

In order to detect if the API *full-screen* is available and the page can be shown in full screen we will use the following code:

```
function fullscreenEnabled() {
    return document.fullscreenEnabled ||
```

```
        document.webkitFullscreenEnabled ||
        document.mozFullScreenEnabled ||
        document.msFullscreenEnabled;
};
if (fullscreenEnabled()) {

    ....

}
```

Note that according to the browser, '*screen*' is written with the first letter as a capital letter '*S*'. This is because during the initial specifications the *API* was defined with the first letter as a capital. This point was changed in the final version.

Changing to full screen mode

Before requesting the full screen mode, we must figure out what method the browser recognises. For this we have created a function that determines the correct method and invokes it.

```
function fullscreen(element) {
    if (!element) element=document.documentElement;
    element.requestFullscreen = element.requestFullscreen ||
        element.mozRequestFullScreen ||
        element.webkitRequestFullscreen ||
        element.msRequestFullscreen;
    element.requestFullscreen();
}
```

Now it's only necessary to call the function with the element that we want to maximise.

```
// To see the page in full screen
fullscreen();
```

```
// For an image, for example to the event onclick
fullscreen(document.getElementById("mi_imagen"));
```

Cancelling full screen mode

Cancelling full screen mode also requires the browser manufacturer prefixes, for which we will use the same idea from the previous section and create a function that will determine what method to use.

```
function exitFullscreen() {
    document.exitFullscreen = document.exitFullscreen ||
        document.mozCancelFullScreen ||
        document.webkitExitFullscreen ||
        document.msExitFullscreen;
```

```
    document.exitFullscreen();
}
exitFullscreen();
```

Verifying if full screen mode is active

With the property *document.fullscreenElement* can we not only determine what element we will find maximised, but we can also detect if it is activated in full screen mode. For this we only have to verify if its value is *null*.

The version for multiple browsers is as follows:

```
function isInFullscreenMode() {
    return document.fullscreenElement ||
        document.webkitFullscreenElement ||
        document.mozFullScreenElement ||
        document.msFullscreenElement;
}

function toggleFullscreen() {
    if (isInFullscreenMode()) {
        exitFullscreen();
    } else {
        fullscreen();
    }
}
```

Capturing full screen events

The capture of events with the browser's prefixes is as follows:

```
function init () {
    if (fullscreenEnabled()) {
        document.getElementById("supported").innerHTML="HTML5 Fullscreen API is available ";
        document.getElementById("supported").style.color="green"
        handlerScreenChange ();
    } else {
        document.getElementById("supported").innerHTML=" HTML5 Fullscreen API is not available";
        document.getElementById("supported").style.color="red"
    }
}
document.addEventListener("fullscreenchange", handlerScreenChange);
document.addEventListener("webkitfullscreenchange", handlerScreenChange);
document.addEventListener("mozfullscreenchange", handlerScreenChange);
document.addEventListener("MSFullscreenChange", handlerScreenChange);
```

CSS pseudo-class :fullscreen

A CSS pseudo-class called "*:fullscreen*" has been included with this JavaScript API that allows us to customise any element when full screen is active. For example, with the following code we indicate that the image with the id "*demo-img*" should display a red frame with a blue background.

```
<style>
    .demo-img:fullscreen {
        padding:42px;
        background-color: blue;
        border:2px solid #f00;
    }
    .demo-img:-webkit-full-screen {
        padding:42px;
        background-color: blue;
        border:2px solid #f00;
    }
    .demo-img:-moz-full-screen {
        padding:42px;
        background-color: blue;
        border:2px solid #f00;
    }
    .demo-img:-ms-fullscreen {
        padding:42px;
        background-color: blue;
        border:2px solid #f00;
    }
</style>
...
<img class="demo-img" src="..\data\graphics\portraits\male_magician.png" onclick="fullscreen(this)">
...
```

C6 THREEJS: UPCOMING BOOKS IN THE COLLECTION

So, our game is starting to come to life, but we are still far from the end and we still have many issues to deal with and some of them are basic ones:

Management of collision detection: if we look at the last example we've presented, as we move around the map we see how we can go through the walls, villagers and even monsters. This behaviour is unthinkable in a real game, so we must implement a strategy to detect when two objects will collide with each other. The simplest way to do this would be to calculate if a vertex of an object is inside another. Unfortunately, this method is not feasible due to the high calculation cost. Remember that we must respond in a few thousandths of a second to get closer to 60 frames per second. Therefore, the solution is to create simpler alternatives figures, wrapping objects in planes, cubes or spheres and calculating intersections based on these figures.

I've attached a picture, which we'll open the second book as this is where we'll learn this technique. In the photo, I've forced imaginary cubes to be represented. This makes it easier to see the final result while developing the examples.

Fig. 6.1. Example of collision detection

Motor of physical laws: Another important part of simulating a scene and games inspired by the real-world are physical laws, such as gravity, acceleration, or friction. This involves determining how objects react to pushing, hitting or exposure to gravity. Imagine a board full of dominos strategically placed one after another, and that the rest will fall one by one by pushing one down, or the movement of fabric in the wind, that changes its surface.

To implement all this is a very complex task. Fortunately, there are many libraries that deal with writing the laws of physics, which make the task child's play. Typically, we'll resort to the representation of objects with simpler shapes, such as cubes, planes, spheres, etc., to reduce the calculations, as we did for detecting collisions. In fact, it's common to use physical laws simulation libraries to detect collisions.

By using this technique, we can represent a house by using a cube, for example. Moreover, if you throw a ball against the surface of the house, the way it bounces off it is calculated considering only the cube, instead of worrying about the relieves of the house, windows, etc.

Creating a rich interface for the game: At the beginning of the book I showed some pictures of the final game. Among those included were the inventory management window, the character tab, the start menu and portraits of the group of adventurers on the screen. But in the book, I've not referred to it again. I've only given some tips on how to build the interface, such as when I explained how to create a box with statistics, when I specified how to add a progress bar or when discussing the use of the class *THREE.Sprite*. In the next book, we'll see how to make menus, inventory windows and add floating labels on the characters and objects.

Fig. 6.2. Example of creating an interface for the game.

Management of sound effects and background music: one issues I've not covered in this book is that of sound effects in the game. This includes the noise produced by striking an enemy, the buzz when casting a spell or background conversations in a tavern. Sounds may come from different distances and, as we move nearer to or further away from the source of the noise, the volume should be adjusted gradually. Distant sounds should be more muted, while closer ones must be louder. Furthermore, a slightly different sound should be generated by the right speaker in relation to the left depending if the sounds come from the far right or left.

Therefore, we'll learn how to handle different channels of audio and mix them together so that the different sounds and effects unite into one, because we only have one audio output.

The other point to explore is learning how to select background music that creates an atmosphere and changes if we are in a dark cave or in a lively village. As I've said before, the music should be mixed with background sounds to produce a single output.

How to store and retrieve data items: playing a role play game involves many hours, so it's necessary to save the stage of the game to subsequently restore it. This involves saving the state of the characters, their level, their location, the changes that have taken place on the map, the mission diary and plot advancement. There are many options for storing data on the internet, such as storing it on a centralized server and sending information through AJAX calls, or by taking advantage of the power offered by Web technologies to store data locally: *localStorage*, *IndexedDB* and *WebSQL*.

How to package and distribute our application: a very important decision is how to distribute our creations. For example, will it be embedded in a web page or will it be an application packaged as ready to distribute in apps stores for *Mac, Windows,* or for *Google store* or the *Apple Store*. So, we must consider what platforms they will be run on. For instance, we must decide if they will only be accessible from the desktop or if they will be also being accessible from phones and tablets.

In future books, we'll not only see how to include them on a webpage, but also how to package them as applications for distribution on mobile phones and tablets using ***PhoneGap***.

We'll also learn to use cache to allow applications to run offline. The ***AppCache*** is a mechanism included in *HTML5* which allows web-based applications to run offline. Developers can use the interface ***Application cache (AppCache)*** to specify the resources that the browser must save in the cache so that they can be accessed without connecting to the internet.

Improving the Artificial Intelligence of monsters and villagers: in Chapter Four we've seen two very basic forms of artificial intelligence to give villagers seemingly intelligent behaviour and to make the monsters move in a confined given area. But frankly, this is far from what may be considered to be artificial intelligence. In the next books, we'll discuss algorithms to find a route between two points, considering the specifics of the terrain and obstacles on the map.

Another point is how to manage our enemies' range of vision, so that they attack only when we enter their field of vision, taking into consideration obstacles, and hiding places. In this way, we can hide behind rocks and walls to simulate a stealthy attack.

Another important point for role playing games is the reaction of the characters in conversation and the reactions of the player. This will also be analyzed in future books.

Sharders, advanced textures and particle system: In the *Three.js* library there remain important points to explore. We'll learn what *Sharders* are and how to use them to effectively alter the vertices and textures. For example, to add bulk to a plane and create mountains and valleys with the technique of *Heightmaps*.

Another point to consider is the advanced use of textures, from using *Bump mapping* to provide relieves, folds and making objects rough without the need to increase the number of polygons, to even creating animated textures and using video to generate them.

Particles are a feature in common with video games where we try to recreate all kinds of explosion in each situation. In fact, we can represent a variety of other physical phenomena, such as smoke, moving water, rainfall, etc. through simulation of a particle system. In the next books, we'll discuss the system included in *Three.js*.

3D animated models: In this book, we've seen how to use previously constructed 3D animated models and to activate their animation. We've introduced the two main techniques to animate characters and figures, for transformation(*morph*) and through a skeleton. In future books, we'll explore these methods in more detail and learn how to use *Blender* to create 3D models and animations, by providing them with skeletons.

You can see how the development of the game and the collection of books are going, read articles and tutorials on animation and programming for the WEB, as well as access various free resources, such as examples in the books and 3D models ready to use in your projects on https://www.thefiveplanets.org.